iGod

RETHINKING OUR LIFE STORY

DR. GREG W. MITCHELL

iGod – Rethinking Our Life Story

© 2013 by Greg W. Mitchell. First printed 2013. This edition 2018.
Published by Greg W. Mitchell
536 East 53rd Avenue
Vancouver, BC V5X 1J5
Canada

Email   greg.mitchell@everynation.org
Website   12-2resources.com

Printed by CreateSpace, An Amazon.com Company

Library and Archives Canada Cataloguing in Publication

Mitchell, Greg W., 1961-, author
    iGod : rethinking our life story / Greg W. Mitchell.

Includes bibliographical references.
Issued in print and electronic formats.
ISBN 978-0-9920642-0-4 (pbk.).--ISBN 978-0-9920642-1-1 (pdf)

    1. Bible--Theology. 2. God--Love. I. Title.

BS543.M58 2013   230'.041   C2013-906101-0
                                              C2013-906102-9

Cover design: Jonathan Mitchell
Illustrations: Dala Botha
Editing: Cathy Reed and Marianne Mendgen

Recommendations

When you have a church movement that has over 6,000 small group leaders and over 72,000 in attendance, you need to have simple concepts that can be duplicated. More importantly, they cannot just be simple; they must be theologically sound. This is what Greg Mitchell has done for our churches in Metro-Manila. His ideas and teaching have helped us further empower our members, the impact of which will only be determined in heaven.

Joey Bonifacio, *Senior Pastor, Victory Christian Fellowship, Fort Bonifacio, Metro-Manila*

Greg Mitchell is one of those modern-day theologians who is able to make things simple and easy to understand. He reminds me of people like William P. Young, Philip Yancey and Eugene Peterson. Greg has ministered in our churches and made a profound impact. His understanding of love, grace, and truth is rich. He lives what he teaches, and teaches in a way that makes it easy for you to put it into practice. I wholeheartedly recommend Greg and his ministry.

Gareth Stead, *Lead Elder, His People Christian Church, Cape Town, South Africa*

I worked with Greg for several years on a project to create an international leadership training curriculum. During that time, he impressed me with his unique ability to cut through the clutter surrounding important biblical issues and to strike at the heart of the matter.

Paul Barker, *Director of Leadership Development, Every Nation Ministries*

Greg Mitchell is a man who is characterized by his warmth, and who has transmitted to me God's wisdom, truth and love. His teachings bring much freedom, as they are filled with authenticity and Biblical truth that inspire everyone to be better and to transmit that to others.

Claudio Zolla, *Senior Minister for the Campeones para Cristo Churches, Lima, Peru*

As a pastor in one of the least churched areas in North America, we've experienced the challenges of reaching and discipling diverse people. Dr. Greg Mitchell's book *iGod* is an accessible and holistic synthesis of theology and life practice. Of all the theological grids I've experienced, Greg's has not only been the most personally edifying; it has also produced the best quantitative and qualitative results in discipleship.

Seth Trimmer, *Lead Pastor, Grace City, Corvallis, Oregon*

Teachers have a God graced ability to find unique ways to explain, enlighten and apply truth to life's reality. Good teachers, however, go well beyond their love of scripture and gifting; they are constantly asking themselves if people are incarnating these truths. But great teachers go even further; their very life's journey reflects the reality of the truths they so carefully share with others. Greg is such a teacher. His gifting is obvious, but it's his humility and authentic journey of faith that inspire observers, readers and listeners alike to eagerly lean into the truths he shares and lives so transparently. Not only has our church community been altered in profound ways by Greg's teaching; so have all the churches he has served in our nation—and around the globe.

Brant Reding, *Canadian Director, Every Nation Ministries*

Dr. Greg Mitchell has had a profound impact on our local church. His ability to apply the truths of God's Word to the deepest issues of the human heart in such a clear and understandable way has brought tremendous growth to the lives in our church. Greg's penetrating insight into the Word of God coupled with his warm and engaging personality makes for a powerful and relatable presentation of truth that genuinely leads to life change.

Nik Harrang, *Pastor, Every Nation Church, Seattle, Washington*

Greg Mitchell is a man with a great love for people, the local church, and most importantly the Lord. He is a gifted teacher and able to make complex subjects simple and understandable. He has authored materials that we have used with great effectiveness in training over half a million House Church leaders in China. He has both written and taught on leadership, discipleship, counseling, theology, and family. Greg is a person that is warm, engaging, curious, intelligent, and passionate about the Kingdom. I endorse both him and his ministry.

Rich Kao, *President, Strategic China Initiative*

(Note: these endorsements of the author do not necessarily imply an agreement with every theological position outlined in this book.)

Thank you to my Every Nation and local church families; you have shaped me and turned my rough ideas into living experiences.

Debbie, during the countless hours I spent writing this book, you were living it out. Thank you for being my inspiration, my best friend, and a safe place.

Jonathan, Eunice, Toby, Tyler, Jessica, Naomi, Noah, Isaac, Yemill, and Jonah:
Mom and I dedicate this book to your future. We pray that the God described in these pages will overflow in your life.

Table of Contents

Introduction
A Love Story

Storyline

If I asked you to describe the reasons behind your personal struggles or why you haven't fully realized your dreams, what would you answer? Perhaps you would outline a series of unfortunate circumstances. Maybe you would describe the need for a better skill set. You might even speak of inner turmoil, like depression or anxiety, which steals away your drive. All these answers are legitimate, but this book addresses the question by looking at the *source* of our struggles.

To explain where our struggles originate, I want to use the idea of "story." Think of yourself as a young actor who has a series of upcoming auditions. It is time for your first interview, and you arrive in full character. You are trying out for a zombie role in a horror film so you dress the part, memorize every line, and understand your motivation, only to realize that this audition is for a romantic comedy. You are fully prepared… for the wrong storyline.

Now think of your own life. What if your problems or disappointments are not primarily about bad circumstances, underdeveloped skills, or inner struggles? What if they stem from not knowing the right storyline (or that a storyline even exists)? Like a zombie in a romantic comedy, you are destined for frustration and failure simply because you have a wrong set of assumptions about your life's story. You are a character in pursuit of a story that can adequately explain the meaning of life and the role you play in it. This is where the road begins to finding true and lasting fulfillment.

Bored

So what, then, is the story that can redefine our lives? Simply stated, it is a love story. As I imagine people's reaction to that statement, I picture at least three responses. Group One is already bored. Filled with images of chick-flicks and group hugs, love is a mushy idea. To this group I hope to show how love is *the* solution to life's problems.

Three stories topped today's news headlines: the arrest of an ex-porn star turned murderer who sent the body parts of his dismembered victim through the mail, the government's plan to fight human trafficking, and the latest on Europe's economic crisis. These issues might seem unrelated until we see that behind every act of violence, perversion, or greed is a life that has not been properly marinated in love. When love is not adequately woven into the fabric of people's lives, they become part of the problem.

My experience confirms this. Not only does being a pastor give me a window into people's lives, my wife Debbie and I have opened our home to people from many backgrounds. We've seen that without a proper foundation of love, people become deformed and destructive. With love, however, people are better, even amidst dreadful conditions.[1] Love is the primary quality that shapes us.

When we weigh the critical nature of love against people's experience of love, it is not overstating to say that our society is in a

---

[1] See Viktor Frankl's experience in World War II concentration camps. Viktor E. Frankl, *Man's Search for Meaning* (Boston: Beacon Press, 1959).

relational crisis. Look at parenting for example. One in three children in America is raised in a fatherless home. Statistics say that these children are five times more likely to commit suicide, twenty times more likely to have behavioral disorders, fourteen times more likely to commit rape, nine times more likely to drop out of school, ten times more likely to abuse substances, and twenty times more likely to go to prison.[2] When love suffers, the resulting physical, emotional, economic, and social cost is limitless.

No amount of legislation, funding, or positive feelings can offset the need to build our lives and relationships upon the foundation of love. This book's focus on love, then, is more than a mushy idea; it presents a core solution to the problem of evil.

Skeptical

Group Two is skeptical because I've reduced the complexity of life to such a simple solution. Oversimplification is a real danger, but so is missing the point. For example, which is more valuable: the self-sacrifice of a mother, or beating a video game? Not all pursuits are of equal worth. At the end of the day, the degree of love in a thing or an action determines its ultimate value.

We might describe love differently, or even doubt its existence, but we all have a sense that love is the highest good. This means that what makes a thought or action helpful or harmful is how much it promotes or undermines love. Love gives us a way not just to evaluate ourselves; it gives humanity a common criterion by which to discern good and bad. As simple as it is, love is the universal standard of morality.

---

[2] http://www.afmus.org/nav_fatherlessfamilies.html. 06/12.
http://www.fathermag.com/news/1780-stats.shtml. 02/06.

Even those who believe in a specific religion must submit to this criterion. As a Christian, I must not raise my beliefs above this standard, for how many times have people used the Bible to justify atrocities? Accepting or rejecting a belief system must be based solely upon whether it is the most loving.

Saying that love is *the* criterion by which to evaluate thoughts and actions is a bold statement. That is why the rest of this book seeks to support this proposition. My goal is to show how love is the best story, the highest good, the ideal solution, the universal truth, the most accurate way to make sense of God and life. My hope is to show how love must be *the* ideal toward which we build our lives.

Distracted

Group Three agrees with the Beatles that love is all we need, but they can't see how it practically changes their lives. After all, love doesn't pay the bills or lower our cholesterol. When we can't picture how love is useful, it is tempting to settle for more concrete life purposes. We go to school, pursue success, get fit, find a cause, and hope no one asks a deeper question.

While some might achieve these goals, we all know that the externals of life do not compensate for a hollow heart. Unattractive people don't necessarily have worse marriages, and smart or funny people aren't always happier, but as someone said, "Research says we can't buy happiness, but can I be in the next test group?" We can hope that such things will deliver on their promises, but we must not distract ourselves from the fact that only a love-filled life is truly meaningful.

Therefore, the final goal of this book is to reveal the practical power of love. It is one thing to describe a story that promotes love as the best idea, but unless it has the power to change our own life stories, it is a fairy tale. So I am eager to share with you, not a theory that has entertained my mind, but a reality that has transformed my life.

You Are Invited

Have you ever tried doing a jigsaw puzzle without a picture to reference? Talk about frustrating! It grieves me to see many of us working hard to piece our lives together without a quality picture to guide us. We collect ideas or experiences in the hope of creating a satisfying life, but the result is less than ideal.

I get particularly upset when we get told that there is no big picture or storyline at all; life is simply what we make of it. More than cruel, it is not true. There is a big idea, a guiding light, a life purpose, a true story that can explain life, and it can be summed up in one word: love.

Imagine each of the following chapters as pieces of a puzzle. As each chapter answers a key question from a love perspective, a picture will form that shows the completeness and power of love. This book, then, is a thorough and consistent presentation on love and its source. So, even if you are bored, skeptical, or distracted, I pray that you will take the time to read on. You have a rare chance to do more than tweak your life; you have an opportunity to change it.

So you're invited. You are invited to stretch yourself into considering what might very well be a new life storyline. What an exciting opportunity! Ready? Here we go.

Chapter One
A True Story

Source

There is a good reason why we are fascinated with love stories—we hope they're true. Even if the story is an action thriller, after all the twists and turns and explosions, we want the good guy to win. Something in us wants justice to succeed and love to be true. Sadly, however, it is easy to settle in our minds that justice is only achieved on the big screen, and love only wins in novels. Is there a love story that is truly true… for us? For love to graduate beyond the realm of fantasy or entertainment, it must be grounded in truth.

If love is the great ideal, the first question we need to ask is: where do we find the truth about love? We could follow our hearts, but that has gotten us into all kinds of trouble. We could poll "the people," but history has proven that popular opinion doesn't make something right. Maybe we should study every belief system and pick a winner, but this is impossible: there are too many religions and philosophies to ever make an educated decision.

There is a better and easier way to find the truth about love. Rather than beginning with the *content* of truth, begin with its *source*. Source always precedes content, for any story or idea is only as good as its source—ask a journalist or judge. This is why I never ask a plumber about my toothache. Nor do I seek counsel from my dentist when our toilet floods. Just as in academics, where the quality of a paper is determined by the quality of its references, so the quality of a story is determined by the quality of its source.

A quest for truth, then, should start with the question: "Is my source of truth worthy of my trust?" The discovery of truth is always about trusting someone or something to be a qualified source. Truth and trust are bound to each other. If I ask someone for directions and follow their advice, I trusted them. If I believe a news report, it is because I trust their sources. If I doubt what everyone else says and trust only in myself, I am still exercising trust. It's unavoidable.

Unless we examine the trustworthiness of our sources, content is a distraction. When a witness in a court of law is discredited, why bother hearing what they say? Source is always our first concern. Fortunately, although the number of beliefs is endless, the number of sources is limited to three: human, natural, and divine. Which are trustworthy?

Human

People are easily the most common source of truth in which we trust, and the person we prefer to trust most is *self*. For many today, truth is what "I" think and feel, and so my highest goal is to be "true to myself." As common as this is, we are unreliable sources of truth for at least three reasons.

First, we are *ignorant*. Imagine a circle inside which are all the things that could ever be known. Now shade in the circle according to how much *you* know (be sure to use a fine-tipped pen). It is staggering to consider how little we know.

> There is a way which seems right to a man, but its end is the way of death. (Proverbs 14:12)

What's worse is that we don't know what we don't know. Which I'm pretty sure is a lot… but I don't really know. The reality is, what we call convictions are best described as guesses. What's worse, we are prone to twisting facts to fit our agendas, thus turning truths into errors (which is why we doubt medical research sponsored by tobacco companies).

When human reason is the benchmark for understanding, statistical probability replaces truth, and rightly so, because this is the best we can expect from people. The logic breaks down, however, when we think that just because *we* can't be certain, truth does not exist.

Second, we are *sinful*. We do wrong things all the time. Even our good actions often have mixed motives, and good excuses don't turn a wrong into a right (just ask the victim of a drunk driver). As my friend Paul Barker says, "Everyone cheats." No one is perfectly consistent in living out their own beliefs, let alone following God's standards.

While it should be easy to admit we're imperfect (at least theoretically), it is harder to see how our wrongdoing distorts our thoughts. Maybe we can see how children manipulate truth to justify their actions: "I had to hit him—he took my toy!" As we grow up, our justifications may have more syllables, but they are just as deceptive: "But officer, considering my physical surroundings and emotional state… ." As much as we hope it isn't true, no one is purely logical. We all bend and twist reason to fit our personal agendas.

It follows that our beliefs about God are shaped more by our morality than our rationality. We typically reverse engineer: we start with the way we want to live, and then work backwards to construct beliefs to support that lifestyle: "What the heart loves, the will chooses, and the mind justifies."[3]

Humanist Aldous Huxley confesses exactly this:

> I had motives for not wanting the world to have meaning, consequently assumed that it had none, and was able without any difficulty to find satisfying reasons for this assumption.... . For myself, as no doubt for most of my contemporaries, the philosophy of meaninglessness was essentially an instrument of liberation. The liberation we desired was simultaneous liberation from a certain political and economic system, and liberation from a certain system of morality. We objected to the morality because it interfered with our sexual freedom.[4]

I remember when our oldest son was about two. He would cover himself with a blanket and quietly shuffle into the room where Debbie and I were sitting. We would smile at each other and say, "Where's Jonathan? I can't see him anywhere!" The blanket would start to jiggle with laughter, and then in one sweeping movement he would reveal himself. We would jump in surprise, and ask him how he got into the room without us noticing.

This picture mimics the blinding nature of sin. Blankets of reasons that we use to justify our sinful actions blind us to the truth. We think that because we can't see truth, it doesn't exist. This is especially true about God. Somehow we think that our blindness proves he isn't real. Certainly, morality isn't the only thing that shapes reason, but if we were less self-centered, it would be easier to see truth.

Third, we are *weak*. Our scientific, athletic, and social achievements give cause for optimism, but we have inflated our potential to the point of lying. We tell children that they can be and do anything. We comfort sinners by assuring them that they really

---

3 Ashley Null, quoted by Mike Wilkerson, *Redemption* (Wheaton: Crossway, 2011), 125.

4 Aldous Huxley, *Report,* "Confession of a Professed Atheist," June 1966.

are good. We tell thousands that they can be the best, knowing that this promise can only be true for one.

I fear that success blinds us to our weakness as much as sin blinds us to reason. A medical doctor told me what inflated confidence looks like in some of his middle-aged male patients. He and his colleagues call it "boomer-itis." It afflicts them with the belief that they can do whatever their younger counterparts can. The resulting torn x and broken y speak otherwise.

In contrast, reality helps restore our sight. It can show us the true extent of our limitations. A degenerating body is just the beginning. We can't control the past. We don't know the future. We can't even control ourselves. Our addictive and destructive tendencies, added to our psychological and physical limitations, multiplied by our track record of relational discord, more than cancel out the other side of the invincibility equation. What is most disturbing is that we can't control what happens after the grave (a concern that is best not ignored).

No matter how often people tell us to believe in ourselves, our ignorance, sinfulness, and weakness make us unworthy sources of truth. Moreover, any other person—whether they are a lover, expert, or guru—suffers from the same limitations that we do. History proves that placing our ultimate trust in people is unwise, for the most frequent results are disappointment and hurt.

Natural

If people cannot be the ultimate source of truth, perhaps something outside humanity is better. The first of these external options is *natural*, meaning things like knowledge, nature, or money. Here we trust that the laws of nature, logic, or success will satisfy us, and it is often true. We find clarity in logic, health through science, quiet in nature, and enjoyment through money.

What is wrong with these benefits? At one level, nothing, but these sources are unable to lead us to life's goal: love. If trusting people leads to hurt, trusting the impersonal world of thoughts and things leads to a cold, heartless existence. Facts don't love you. Money can't keep you warm at night. Nature can be heartless. They might teach you a lot, but true love isn't one of them.

This is the bind: trusting in people brings pain; trusting in impersonal things leaves us cold. Neither speaks the truth about unconditional love. There is only one more option.

God

If neither nature nor people are adequate sources of truth, the only remaining option is supernatural. So the question is: if gods are the ultimate source of truth, then which one(s) should we trust? From the thousands of Hindu gods to the one Muslim god to every other option, looking for a single source of truth seems to be a complicated pursuit. So where do we start? Let's recap the ground rules:

a) Since life's ultimate purpose is love, then the ultimate source of truth must lead us there.

b) The source has to be both trustworthy (not flawed), and personal (not cold). If either of these qualities is missing, then that god can't teach us about love.

Love is the perfect way to evaluate deities. If gods are distant, singular, or simply a force, they lack the warmth of love (they can't teach us about something they aren't). If they are self-serving, brutal, mute, or non-sacrificial, they too are disqualified. If they demand payment for blessing, move on (why trust someone like that?). It doesn't matter what we grew up believing, or what is convenient to believe; have the courage to find a god that captures the fullness of love.

Here is the shocking truth: the benchmark of love narrows down the field to just one—Jesus Christ. How can such a simplistic declaration be made? We can summarize the uniqueness of Jesus among all sources in three statements: Jesus is God, he came to earth, and he rose from the dead. We will examine these in greater detail later, but here is a summary:

Jesus

Jesus is God (John 1:1). While prophets and sages claim to *know* the truth, Jesus claims to *be* the truth for he is God (John 14:6). Truth is not an abstract list of facts, nor a subjective collection of experiences; truth is a *person*. To know Jesus is to know the truth. How comforting! Our search for truth doesn't end with an idea or a feeling; it ends with a relationship. This kind of truth satisfies, for it answers the questions of both mind *and* heart.

Jesus came to earth as a man (John 1:14). The best other religions provide is a road map to somewhere. In contrast, Jesus came to us— the person became personal. Therefore, the purpose of life is not to find the truth, because the Truth found us. This means that finding truth is not a future goal; it is a present reality. Jesus Christ physically revealed God to us, removing the speculative nature of truth finding. The truth we see is a God who is neither uncaring nor impotent, for Jesus entered our broken world to give us new life in him.

Jesus rose from the dead (Luke 24:46-47). The love that Jesus demonstrated on earth culminated in his death and resurrection. This means that his truth is not just better ideas; it is a real event that saves us *from* death and *into* eternal life with him and his community.

This description of Jesus reveals that truth is not sterile, legalistic, abstract, or impersonal. It is love—a real, costly, mysterious, personal, effective, beautiful, humbling love. A love so valuable, it can only be described as salvation.

While we stumble around in ignorance, sinfulness, and weakness, inventing stories to explain our existence, Jesus enters our world as all-knowing, all-loving, and all-powerful. His truth does more than just inspire or enlighten; he has the power to bring us into a love relationship with God and each other. When love is the measure of truth, Jesus wins.

How does Jesus continue to be our truth? Now that he has left this earth and returned to heaven, how does he continue to help us know and follow the right storyline? He does it through his Word (the Bible) and by his Spirit. This is how Jesus stays personal.

The Bible

By giving us the Christian Bible, Jesus gave us an objective means of knowing him—he wrote his story down (2 Timothy 3:16). The purpose of the Bible is to reveal God and how we can rightly relate to him.[5] It is unique among literature because it claims to be divinely inspired.

The debates are endless about whether today's Bible is true to the original manuscripts, or whether its human writers misrepresented the "real" Jesus. But ultimately, the real issue is again about source. Either we trust that Jesus is able to reveal himself, or we trust in the opinion of some historian who wasn't there and is barely here. A little humility would go a long way in this regard. I am indebted to the work of academics, but they cross a line if they *define* instead of *discover* truth.

Ultimately, we trust the Bible's story because we trust in its divine author.[6] We do not trust in new ideas or old suspicions about

---

[5] "The Bible is a record of a relationship between God and man." Gerald Bray, *God is Love* (Wheaton: Crossway Books, 2012), 11.

[6] As important as historical evidence is, we must admit its limitations. N.T. Wright, in describing the evidence for the resurrection, says, "We cannot use a supposedly

the Bible because that would imply that God is neither willing nor able to communicate with us. If God's Word is not reliable, then neither is God; if God isn't trustworthy, then an unreliable Bible is the least of our problems. Instead, as we base our confidence in the Bible on *his* faithfulness rather than *our* understanding, even our questions become avenues of discovery.

To trust in the Bible's divine inspiration means believing that its truth is *plenary* (the complete Bible), *verbal* (inspired words, not just ideas), *authoritative* (not one of many sources of truth), and *inerrant* (without error).[7]

> The inerrancy of the Bible means simply that the Bible tells the truth. Truth can and does include approximations, free quotations, language of appearances, and different accounts of the same event as long as those do not contradict.[8]

We read the Bible objectively by seeking something called the *original intent*. We ask, "What was God telling *them*?" before asking, "What is God telling *us*?" We find the original intent by applying

---

objective historical epistemology as the ultimate ground for the truth of Easter. To do so would be like lighting a candle to see whether the sun had risen.... All knowing is a gift from God, historical and scientific knowing no less than that of faith, hope, and love; but the greatest of these is love." N. T. Wright, *Surprised by Hope* (HarperCollins e-books, 2008), 73-74.

[7] "Canon" refers to those books that are believed to be authored by God. The canon developed slowly, but the Synod of Hippo (393 AD) affirmed the 27 books of the New Testament. (F.F. Bruce, *The Books and the Parchments*, 113). Four main tests determined New Testament canonicity: 1. The author was an apostle or had connection with an apostle; 2. The church at large accepted it; 3. Its content reflected orthodox teaching; 4. It reflected the moral and spiritual quality of inspiration. The early church rejected the Apocrypha as canon because it was not part of the Jewish Scriptures, it had historical inaccuracies, it did not reflect Biblical teaching or spirituality, and Jesus never quoted it.

[8] Charles C. Ryrie, *What You Should Know About Inerrancy*, 16. "Language of appearances" means that the authors spoke about what they saw, not necessarily what something really is.

standard principles of interpretation: we appreciate historical context, literary conventions, language, situational versus ideal morals,[9] and the tension of paradoxical truths.[10] Through proper study, we seek to reposition ourselves to see God's written story from *his* perspective instead of *our* self-centered biases or opinions. While we are never completely free from bias, integrity and humility enable us to see the Bible for what it is: a true story.

How valuable it is to have a reliable source of truth! The Bible is a rudder, mirror, sword, anchor, light, compass, lens, and food. While the subjectivity of human ideas is shifting sand, we have a rock that is timeless and unshakeable. Without the Bible, we are lost in a sea of human opinions. With the Bible, we can understand reality from God's viewpoint, which moves love beyond sentiment to a solid foundation.

The Spirit

While the Bible is an amazing gift, all is not bliss in the land of objective truth. Instead of worshipping Jesus as the truth, some people worship the Bible itself (John 5:39-40). Have you ever met people who are vending machines of Biblical truth: ask a question and out pops a Bible verse? I think they're trying to be helpful, but

---

[9] Not every Bible verse presents God's moral ideal (Mt.5:21ff). Like a parent correcting his son, sometimes God only gives the next step toward the ideal. For example, the Old Testament's view of slavery surpassed the surrounding cultures' views; the New Testament went further, but the trajectory of Scripture continues with Wilberforce's abolition of one human owning another in 1807. William J. Webb, *Slaves, Women and Homosexuals* (Downers Grove: InterVarsity Press, 2001).

[10] Some truths seem paradoxical: Is Jesus God or man? Is God merciful or just? Are we in control or is God? Faulty thinking can reduce truth to either *x* or *y*, or a little of both. Klaus Bockmuehl taught me Barth's approach to Bible study—called *dialectical theology*. It holds truths in tension, like Jesus is 100% God and 100% man, or life is 100% God-led and 100% our choice.

their "help" leaves me feeling guilty and frustrated. I want to wave my hand over their eyes to find out if they can see that they're talking to a person—a person whose life cannot fit into their wooden answers.

Remember, truth serves a purpose higher than itself. So the dry communication of Biblical facts forgets that the goal of truth is to teach us about love. Likewise, using Bible facts to support loveless choices is equally wrong. If we use, for example, the truth of eternal security to excuse our sin ("I'm guaranteed heaven no matter what I do"), it becomes false. Any truth that twists itself into justifying loveless thoughts or actions twists itself into becoming a lie because the intent of God's truth is always to foster love (1 Timothy 1:5).

When God's story is reduced to a series of facts, the Bible degenerates into being an impersonal source of truth, leaving us cold, alone and divisive.[11] It becomes a book of rules, principles or ideas, rather than a gateway into knowing God. As disturbing as this idea might be for some Christians, the Bible is not enough for us to know the truth. We also need God's Spirit (1 Corinthians 2:11-12).[12]

It takes more than facts to know God; it takes trust. Proof or facts are never perfect enough to remove the need for faith. Why does trust precede truth? Is God being secretive or cruel? No!

---

[11] For example, Christians argue over who determines the future—God or us. One side fights for God's sovereignty; the other side champions our free will. While both sides are biblically supported, people's hostility over the topic of predestination is troubling. A few years ago, at Regent College, I listened to a lecture on John Calvin and why he was an advocate for predestination. It was because the Huguenots feared losing their salvation if they denied Christ while being tortured. So Calvin sought to comfort them with the assurance that God held them securely in his hand, and that their salvation was solely dependent upon God's choosing, not their performance. Right then, I was struck by the contrast between Calvin's compassion and our use of the same truth to judge and divide! Facts alone are not enough to rightly handle truth.

[12] See also John 14:16-18; Luke 24:45.

Remember, truth is a person. He can't show us truth impersonally (which, on its own, is what a holy book is). God speaks in ways that require us to come near, trust, and listen, for only then can he be known. The Bible's story is lifted off of the pages and into our lives when we read it through the lens of trust.

This is what it means to "know" God; the term implies intimacy. You don't know God because you read the Bible any more than you know my children because you can list their ages and eye colors. True knowing moves through facts to intimacy.[13] So if you don't want to know God, no amount of arguments or reason will persuade you to trust in him, no matter how plainly it is written. Thomas Aquinas is quoted as saying, "To one who has faith, no explanation is necessary. To one without faith, no explanation is possible."

We need more than facts to know God. We need his Spirit to warm and instruct our hearts.[14] The most intimate way that God reveals himself to us, then, is through his Spirit. Listen to Jesus' words:

> And I will ask the Father, and he will give you another advocate to help you and be with you forever—the Spirit of truth. The world cannot accept him, because it neither sees him nor knows him. But you know him, for he lives with you and will be in you. I will not leave you as orphans; I will come to you. (John 14:16-18)

What a beautiful promise: God with us! God in us! God's Spirit is not an inanimate force, a spiritual feeling, or a cosmic idea. He is a person whose spirit nature enables him to dwell within us. Distance is removed; love is present, enlightening our minds and comforting

---

[13] "[To] know means intimate knowledge, a living experience, a close relation, and not mere acquaintance or theoretical knowledge about God." R.G. Bratcher & W.D. Reyburn, *A translator's handbook on the book of Psalms* (New York: United Bible Societies, 1991), 347.

[14] Pascal says, "The heart has reasons that reason cannot know." Beauty, romance, self-sacrifice, hope, people… God—there is much of truth that logic cannot fully know.

our hearts, even in the midst of confusion, suffering, or discouragement.

I am overwhelmed by the sweetness of God's presence. My favorite part of the day is when I get to be alone with my heavenly Father. I read his Bible, rest in his presence, and respond back in prayer—prayers that are less about requests and more about connection. In this place, I'm not thinking about proof or theories. The knowledge which I long for is far more intimate than that. This is my place of refuge.

Perhaps some might write off this idea of knowledge as sentimentalism, but I remember looking in the eyes of a wife whose husband prided himself in his logic, which he used to protect himself from hurt. Her sadness revealed his deception. I am that husband, and the most difficult journey of my life has been to come out from the walls of my carefully reasoned defenses to experience love. Whether it is with a spouse or Jesus, we can't know true love until we risk vulnerability.

Conclusion

So as this book attempts to complete a puzzle, the first piece is this: truth is a person—Jesus Christ—who we trust to reveal himself through his Word (the Bible) and by his Spirit. If truth were only subjective, we would wander off in our own thoughts and impressions and leave behind the reality of Christ. If truth were only objective, we would get lost inside facts and miss the person behind the ideas.[15]

---

[15] "The sterile antithesis of 'objective' and 'subjective,' where we say that things are either objectively true (and can be perceived as such by a dispassionate observer) or subjectively true (and so of no use as an account of the real, public world), is overcome by the epistemology of love." *Surprised by Hope*, 73.

Coming to Jesus with *both* our heart and mind helps us to avoid the danger of reducing truth to either a personal experience or a logical fact. We must see that neither feeling nor fact can replace the need for trust. If we use them to avoid instead of build trust, they won't lead us to God, for relationship requires trust. As we trust God's Word to be reliable, understandable, and personal, it comes alive. Trust believes in timeless truth, and then transforms it into intimate knowledge (John 10:3-5, 27). In that place, God's story is seen to be a true story—not only true in terms of verifiable fact, but in terms of encountering the living God.

In this way, we read the Bible relationally, not as fiction or a textbook, for the Bible is a portal into the heart and mind of its divine Author. We do not forsake grammar or historical context, for that would make the Bible (and hence Christ) less objective or certain. Nor do we ignore his Spirit, for true knowledge is intimate. We find Jesus in the midst of a literal and spiritual encounter.

So, will you let truth be personal? Will you use fact and experience to lead you *into* trust, not away from it? Will you not settle for secondhand knowledge but choose to know Jesus yourself? The good news is, God promises to be found by those who seek him (Jeremiah 29:13).

Before we turn to the next chapter, I must be clear: Jesus is the source of truth upon which I seek to base this book's content. It is not enough to explore love from the standpoint of human reason or experience; we must go to love's source. Some people might think I'm being narrow-minded by limiting my exploration of truth to Jesus and his Bible, but we all choose a specific source upon which to base our beliefs. So I've decided to trust in the One who I believe knows the truth about love. With this in mind, let's turn to see what his Bible says about the second puzzle piece: who is the author of our life's story?

Chapter One Discussion Questions

a) Why is *source* more important than *content*? Can you give examples?

b) What kinds of sources of truth, love, and power have you explored? What makes something worthy to be our *ultimate* source?

c) From this chapter, why is Jesus a unique source of truth, love, and power?

d) What kinds of criticism have you heard about the Bible? Who was the source of those criticisms? What must you believe about them and God to respond to what they say?

e) Why does it take more than facts to know God and his love? What undermines our ability to truly "know" God?

Chapter Two
The Author

How

In Chapter One we saw that life's most important question is this: Who is worthy to be trusted? Whose story will we accept as true? Whoever we trust as our source of truth, love, and power is our god, our life's leader.[16]

Choosing our personal leader is the most critical decision we make in life, for the quality of our life is determined by the quality of its leadership. Think of your country, workplace, or home; leadership is the first place to look if there are problems. So it is with us. When we aren't coping with life, we must first ask ourselves: is the one leading my life adequate?

Typically, we don't link our personal problems to who leads our life. We find *how* to be a much more interesting question than *who*. We want to know *how* to have better sex, overcome depression, make money, or improve our golf swing. The problem is, a focus on *how* assumes that *we* are the best leader for our lives. "After all," we say, "who loves me more than I do?" So instead of looking for a qualified leader—one who isn't ignorant, sinful or weak—we tweak our self-leadership skills. We work on relaxing, budgeting, communicating,

---

[16] I am using the words god, leader, creator and author interchangeably, because they all refer to the one who defines us.

dieting, studying, or parenting, all the while assuming *we* should lead our lives.

As beneficial as these exercises are, they do not change who we are—human. No matter how many successes we have in the *hows* of life, they can never offset the need to find the right *who*. Eventually, a circumstance will confront us that an improved golf swing or financial portfolio can't fix. In reality, the only leader qualified to lead our lives (and the world) is divine.

We must accept the truth that, even if we become the best humans possible, we will never be divine. A soccer player who works really hard on his ball handling skills should never be handed a surgeon's scalpel. If the devil worked on self-improvement— relaxing, dieting, communicating, budgeting, and leading—he is still the devil. Any advancements he might make do not change *who* he is; they just help him succeed at *what* he does. The same is true for us. Don't be fooled into thinking that knowing how to cure some diseases, build bridges, or feed the poor can make us God.

Believing this deception is the first sin ever committed. The devil tells Adam and Eve to reject God's leadership by defining life and truth on their own terms (Genesis 3:5). This sounded as good to them as it does to us, and from then on people have resisted God's leadership and put their faith in themselves. But whether it is now or at death, each of us will hit the wall of our humanity.

Given the glaring leadership crisis in our lives, we must take the time to examine who is the true and rightful author of our life story. Don't let yourself be content with distractions. The Allied forces were not working on their golf swing while Hitler was in power. Our present reality is just as dire, so we must humble ourselves before the only God who can rightly lead us.

Who

So let's say that we admit the folly of our leadership and acknowledge that God is our rightful leader. The next question is, who is God? Our answer is vital, because who we believe God to be shapes our life more than any other factor. This is obvious when we observe the unique ways in which people of different religions live out their beliefs. Even if someone doesn't think he is very "spiritual," that belief shapes his values, priorities, decisions, and actions as much as "religious" beliefs do. Our lives always reflect who we think God is and is not.

Moreover, our beliefs about God shape how we read his Bible. If we read it with suspicion and doubt God's motives, we will find more than enough evidence to confirm our suspicions. Just like our ability to hear our spouse is distorted by our beliefs about them, our ability to understand God is shaped by what we believe about him. Our assumptions dramatically shape who we think God is.

Our image of God shapes how we live. This was the conclusion of my Master's thesis: *Who we believe God to be determines how we live.*[17] If we think God is harsh, we live in fear. If we think he is kind, we hedge our bets and party on. If we think he is irrelevant or doesn't exist at all, we live self-made lives. Our theology (our beliefs about God) always expresses itself in how we live.

It follows that our personal problems are rooted in faulty theology (Psalm 115:8). Priest and author Brennan Manning is quoted as saying, "We are shaped by the warped vision of God we have."[18] If we mistrust God's comfort, then chocolate or pornography will be irresistible. If we doubt God's ability to

---

[17] Greg W. Mitchell, *"Come Follow Me!" Discovering Whom we are to Follow in Selected Works of Twentieth Century Protestant Theology* (Vancouver: Regent College, 1988).

[18] Brennan Manning's *The Ragamuffin Gospel* is a must-read for anyone wanting to understand God's love.

reconcile, then division or revenge are our only options. If God isn't our creator, feelings of meaninglessness will be hard to shake. If we believe in karma, personal performance is our master. Theology is practical, for it is the first domino that sets the rest of our life in motion.

Because our lives reflect who we believe God is, then the best way to improve our lives is to improve our knowledge of God. So where are we going to find the truth about who God is? What is the best source? It is God himself.

Asking God is critical, because our personal beliefs are mostly shaped by our personal assumptions and experiences. A study was done on how parents shape their children's view of God.[19] In the study, a test group was asked about their relationship with their parents, and then a few weeks later about their views of God. The following excerpts from various test group participants show the similarity between the two interviews:

BELIEFS ABOUT PARENTS	BELIEFS ABOUT GOD
"I was never close to my father."	"I have never experienced closeness to God."
"My father always insisted I make the most of my abilities."	"If there is a God, then I have dissatisfied him, because I have not made the best use of my abilities."
"I don't ask anything from my father."	"If I am in distress I don't resort to God because I have no belief in God."
"If I could change myself, I would like to be like my mother because I thought she was very strong when I was little."	"For me, my love for God is important because I need him to give me strength."

Our greatest danger is defining God according to our own ideas and experiences—which makes God into something far less than, and different from, who he really is (Isaiah 40:18, 26; Romans 1:25).

---

[19] Ann-Maria Rizzuto, *The Birth of the Living God* (Chicago: University of Chicago Press, 1979), 141, 161.

By way of example, I asked my daughter, who was seven at the time, to draw God. Compare Jessica's drawing with her photograph. God kind of looks like… her!

So how might *you* draw God? When it comes to our images of God, they might be just as sincere but they are just as inadequate. Clearly, the best source for understanding God is himself. Fortunately, God has told us who he is. He has freed us from our ignorance and distortions by defining himself in the Bible. So who does God say he is?

> God has spoken plainly, and I have heard it many times: Power, O God, belongs to you; unfailing love, O Lord, is yours. (Psalm 62:11-12)

The essence of God is captured in two words: love and power. Similarly, Erickson, in his systematic theology, summarizes God according to his goodness and greatness, where goodness defines his character and greatness summarizes his ability.[20] Regardless of the particular words used, these two categories capture all of God's nature: holiness, justice, mercy, wisdom, power, omnipresence, immortality… are all expressions of his love and/or power.

---

[20] Millard J. Erickson, *Christian Theology* (Grand Rapids: Baker, 1998), Ch.13-14.

Interestingly, our criticism of God usually concerns one or both of these attributes. "If God is so loving, why did he command genocide in the Old Testament?" "If God is so powerful, why doesn't he stop human suffering?" These questions reveal the critical nature of these two qualities, for unless God is truly loving and powerful, he cannot be trusted to be our God—so we must be careful to understand these qualities well.

God Is Power

How do you feel when you hear the word *power*? Often we feel suspicion. Whether it is a teacher, parent, priest, or boss, we all have been hurt by authority figures of one kind or another. To minimize the potential for further pain, our natural response is to minimize people's power. Finding support in the adage, "Power corrupts, and absolute power corrupts absolutely," we try to limit the power of leaders. We want them to have enough power to benefit *us*, but not enough to benefit *themselves*. In spite of how hard we try to limit or diversify power, though, we cannot remove it from our experience. Wherever one being influences another, power exists.

While the abuse of authority is wrong, power itself is invaluable. Regardless of the social sphere, we need good leaders—imagine families without parents or classrooms without teachers. So rather than resenting authority, or redistributing power to as many as we can (which multiplies evil instead of extinguishing it), we need someone who can lead us toward a common and greater good. Fortunately, we have such a leader: Jesus Christ.

In the face of our less-than-inspiring experience of authority, Jesus unashamedly announces himself as Sovereign Lord. *Sovereign* means that he has no limitations—not time or space, ability, understanding, powers, or people. Nothing can resist his will (1

Timothy 6:15). He is never confused, afraid, or surprised. Even when Jesus limits himself, he does so out of his own free will.[21]

> [God] does as he pleases with the powers of heaven and the peoples of the earth. No one can hold back his hand or say to him: "What have you done?" (Daniel 4:35b)

His sovereignty is captured in the fact that he is our creator and, as such, exercises complete control over us (Isaiah 40:28; Psalm 135:5-6). As a woodworker, I have built many pieces of furniture; as their creator, I have complete power over their design and use. When it comes to what I've made, I am all-powerful.

We can't change the fact that God is our creator. The question is, how do we respond to him? We could resent God's power and rebel against him, but our personal revolt does nothing to change who he is. As our creator, he owns us. He can't be overthrown; kicking against him only hurts our feet. There is only one appropriate response to this kind of God: fear. As C.S. Lewis writes about the Christ-figure Aslan in *The Lion, the Witch and the Wardrobe*, "He is not a tame lion." He has the power to bless and curse, heal and hurt, save and destroy (James 4:12).

Fear is a disturbing word, for its connotation is typically negative. While it is more comfortable to define fear as respect or awe, fear means exactly what we fear it means: powerlessness, terror, dread. It means realizing that God has the right and the ability to do whatever he wants with us. This is why, like an ant shaking his little fist at us, it is very foolish to defy God. Bravado cannot compensate for size.

---

[21] "*God is sovereign over his sovereignty....* To say that God *can't* be vulnerable, *can't* limit himself, *can't* restrain his power to make room for other powers, is, ironically, to deny God's sovereignty." Roger Olson, "*Relational Theology*," http://www.patheos.com/blogs/jesuscreed/2013/04/17/

As unnerving as it might be to acknowledge that God is all-powerful, it is exactly what we need him to be. Anything less would leave us vulnerable and unprotected. Imagine if we chose the second most powerful god to be our god. What would the first most powerful god do? He'd crush our god and us along with him!

This is why self-worship is so ridiculous. Where do you think *we* rank on the list of all-powerful beings? This is why we feel unsafe and insecure, and why evil ravages us so easily. We are defenseless. It is both unwise and embarrassing to be our own gods. For ultimate safety and peace, it is best to find the most powerful God and submit to him.

Fear was a significant motivation for me becoming a Christian. I didn't fully understand hell but it sounded horrible. So if God could rescue me, I was motivated to get on his good side. Does my fear of God undermine my relational theology? Aren't fear and love opposites? They are not.

An interaction I once had with the police explains why this is so. During my early twenties, I lost my driver's license for a few months because I had so many speeding tickets. I resented the police for doubting my driving skills and limiting my freedom. I felt wronged with each flashing light in my rearview mirror.

Now jump forward a few years to when we invited an addict to live with us. Brian (not his real name) stayed clean for a number of months, but after his first paycheck he shot up with heroin numerous times. We came home that night to find our house ransacked—things were smashed, dented and overturned. I (foolishly) went upstairs to see if Brian was home, and he came out of his room higher than a kite. He became increasingly irate, threatening us, and physically harming another housemate.

In that moment, I did what any manly man would do: I collected my family, ran outside, and phoned 911. The police responded immediately and removed him from our home. So how do you think I felt about the police in that moment? I loved them. The very power that I once resented was now my best friend.

We can treat God the way I treated the police when I was on the wrong side of the law. But rather than resenting his power, or making God smaller or more manageable, it is far better to admit who he is and live on the right side of his power. We need God to be all-powerful or we are hopeless in our weakness. Instead of resenting his power, we should rejoice, for *his* power is *our* security.

Rather than avoiding fear, we must order our fears, for we are controlled by what we fear. The reason we fear people, the future, evil, or the economy, is because we *don't* fear the God who rules those things. When we trust God, however, our fears of lesser things shrink, much the same way we wouldn't be afraid of a bully if we had a bodyguard. Surprisingly, the result of fearing God is fearlessness (Psalm 34:4,7).

God Is Love

If God were *only* all-powerful, we would all be in trouble. Fortunately, God is also pure love. In fact, love doesn't describe God; God describes love. "God is love" (1 John 4:16).

To understand how God is love, we must define what love is for it is a greatly misunderstood term. Some people describe love as a *feeling* or deep attraction but, judging by the mood swings of a teenager, we must pray that love is more than a feeling. True love must run deeper than emotion, otherwise the quality of our relationships is determined by our latest feeling. Can you imagine having parents who love you only when they *feel* like it? We'd all be orphaned by now.

Others describe love as an *action*, which seems better, but it is too naïve to call one behavior always *loving* and another always *unloving.* For instance, is having sex always about making love? Is smiling at your boss always a sign of admiration? Even philanthropy can have mixed motives. Nearly any action can be either good or bad, depending on why we do it. This is why love can't be reduced to a set of rules or laws, for love is first about our hearts, not our actions.

While it includes feelings and actions, the Bible describes love as a *motive*, where we value others over self, and do things for *their* benefit (1 Corinthians 16:14; Philippians 2:3-4).

I saw a wonderful example of this a few years ago when a woman in our church went to volunteer in a South African orphanage. The man who picked her up at the airport eventually became her fiancé. We all looked forward to them coming to Vancouver so we could meet (translation: interrogate) him.

At their engagement party, we asked Bertie to tell us about his relationship with Leslie. He said that the more he got to know her, the more he liked her, so he asked God if she was *the one*. He felt God telling him that he was asking the wrong question, and that a better question would be: "Can you serve this woman for the rest of your life? If you can answer 'Yes' to that question, then she's the one." Bertie spent the next few months determining if he could serve her this way, and as he found joy in doing so, he asked Leslie for her hand in marriage.

After listening to him, we all thought the same thing about him: you're good… really good. What impressed us was that he understood what true love is: serving another for *their* benefit. When I ask college and high school students what the opposite of love is, they always say *hate*. Yet hate and love coexist. For example, I so love my children that I hate pedophiles, or I hate when my kids are unkind. Instead of hate, the opposite of love is *selfishness*. Selfishness and love are mutually exclusive motivations. So the degree to which selfishness motivates us is the degree to which we are not loving others in that moment.

Conversely, when we do something for the sake of another, we love them. It is not about how we *felt* or even exactly what we *did*; it is *why* we did it, or more specifically *for whom* we did it. Love is *selflessness* in its purest form.

Concerning God, when he describes himself as loving, it means that he is perfectly selfless. His only motive is to bless others. Even when he exercises judgment or wrath, or when he tells us to worship him, love is the reason.[22] God is not 99% love and 1% something else, for if love does not define *all* that God is, then we cannot trust in his love. Some people describe God as loving *and* holy, or as seeking love *and* glory, but if love does not motivate all God does, we're in trouble.[23] Like living with an alcoholic, we would never know when we'd see his dark side. Either God is all love, or he can't be trusted. Rather than balancing love with another quality, it is better to gain a better understanding of God's love.

---

[22] "'Wrath' is the best description we have for the way in which God's love encounters sin.… genuine love is positively jealous and protective, for a true lover seeks to defend the love relationship whenever it is threatened by disruption, destruction, or outside intrusion." Stanley J. Grenz, *Created for Community* (Wheaton: BridgePoint, 1996), 48.

[23] Holiness is also about love, as it describes the uniqueness of God, the greatest of which is his love. "… to be holy as God is holy is not simply to be pure and righteous, but to act toward others with purity and goodness, with truthfulness and honesty, with generosity, justice and love… ." R. P. Martin & P.H. Davids, *Dictionary of the Later New Testament and Its Developments* (Downers Grove: InterVarsity Press, 2000).

"*Holy* describes someone or something in a defined relationship. …the point is proper or improper relation to God." David Thompson, quoted by Diane LeClerc, Christianity Today, April, 2014. *The broken, messy—and holy—church.*

"God's holiness is not one of his attributes but his "otherness"—his essential and unique nature, the sum of his sublime attributes." Bruce K. Waltke, CRUX, Winter 2007/Vol. 43, No. 4. 14. *Ask of me, My Son: Exposition of Psalm 2.*

Triune Love

What is a God of love like? As strange as it sounds, God is love because he is Trinitarian: three persons (Father, Son, and Holy Spirit) who are one nature.[24] For years, I thought the Trinity was an awkward truth that I should believe as a Christian. Now, it is at the center of my thoughts about God and life. Why the shift? The Trinity reveals a profound truth: *God is relationship within himself.* Let's unpack this statement.

Relationship requires at least three qualities: *you*, *me*, and *we*. First, relationship or love requires more than one person: it needs a "you." Richard of St. Victor says, "No one is said to have charity on the basis of his own private love of himself."[25] Love does not exist in isolation; it exists in relationship—it must be shared between at least two people. This is why self-love is not a reasonable replacement for being loved by another. We were made for love, and love requires relationship.

Furthermore, for the love of two to be perfected, they must love a third.[26] What an insight! When two people focus only on each other, their love becomes self-serving. True love compels them to care for others, for, by its very nature, love is inclusive.

We see that a higher level of love is required when two goes to three. For example, when one of my children plays with a friend, it usually goes smoothly until a third friend is included. Similarly, some couples choose not to have children because it will disrupt their lives.

---

[24] Matthew 28:19; Deuteronomy 6:4. "The Trinity is composed of three united Persons without separate existence—so completely united as to form one God." Lewis Chafer, *Systematic Theology*, Vol.1, 276.

[25] Richard of St. Victor, Translated by Grover A. Zinn, *The Twelve Patriarchs, The Mystical Ark, Book Three of the Trinity* (New York: Paulist Press, 1979), 374. (Died, 1173AD). "When a plurality of persons is lacking, charity cannot exist." Ibid.

[26] Ibid., 388. "Certainly in only a pair of persons there would be no one with whom either of the two could share the excellent delights of His pleasure." 391.

Others protect themselves from the cost of any kind of intimacy. In contrast, how beautiful is the love in the Trinity! One loves and is loved by a second, who both share their love with a third. There is no hint of selfishness in God.

Therefore, because God is love, he is more than one person. Other core motivations don't require him to be triune. For instance, if the most essential characteristic of God is knowledge, he wouldn't need to be in relation with others—he could be smart on his own. If God was ultimately about power, he wouldn't need others either—the opposite is true because others would threaten his power. Since God is love, he must be in communion with others, for love only exists in relationship.

The second quality of relationship is *me*. Individuality is not lost in a love relationship; instead, who we are is what we give to and receive from others. Unless we take responsibility for our part in a relationship, that relationship is destined to fail. The miracle of the Trinity is that *I* do not lose my self in *you*, for each one uniquely contributes to and benefits from the relationship.[27]

In the Trinity, we do not find the loss of self that we find in a cult or in an enmeshed relationship. Being one God does not make the Trinity less than three selves. This means that there is a difference between self and selfishness. It is not selfish to be unique or to need the love of another. Rather, a healthy sense of self values individuality but sees that it is not an end in itself. We were made to give and receive love.

This brings us to the final quality: *we*. The unity of the persons of the Trinity is so interwoven that they must be described as one

---

[27] "Modern individualism and modern collectivism are mirror images of each other. Both signal the loss of the person, the disappearance of one into the many or the many into the one." Colin E. Gunton, *The Promise of Trinitarian Theology* (Edinburgh: T & T Clark, 1991), 90.

God. What is it that binds all three together? This is interesting because they do not *need* each other in the sense that one is less than another. They are all equally God. The unity of the Trinity only makes sense with one motivation: love.

Their love is so deep, so complete, that they choose to be described by their relationship, not by their individuality. This level of unity does not rob each person of their uniqueness; it fulfills them. They say, "*I need you* to be *me*."[28] Who they are personally can only be defined collectively. God, then, is a perfectly interdependent being—thoroughly in need of another, but never with the loss of self. The shared love of the Father, Son and Spirit makes them who they are: one God, without separation.[29]

Being defined relationally is so contrary to our human impulses. When we want to "find ourselves," we either travel overseas or journey inwardly to explore our hidden self. In either case, we extract ourselves from relationships. Not only is this impossible (we are always a product of our environment, even if we are reacting against it), the self we find is void of love. So, if our ultimate life goal is to be smart, successful, powerful, or happy—travel or meditation might do the trick, but we will never get to love in isolation.

In contrast, God travels in the opposite direction, toward relationship. This helps explain why the Trinity is hidden in the Old Testament. While it is there for the discerning eye to see, no person of the Trinity wants center stage. God weighted the presentation of himself on his unity, not diversity. This reveals how deeply love and relationship define the essence of God.

---

[28]Ibid., 91.

[29] "The three different persons of the Trinity are one not only in purpose and in agreement of what they think, but they are one in essence, one in their essential nature." Wayne Grudem, *Systematic Theology* (Grand Rapids; Zondervan, 1994), 238.

Relationship, then, makes God truly perfect. If love is true perfection, then for God to be perfect he must be love; for love to be his essence, he must be three in one.

All other gods betray love at the core of who they are. The single gods of some religions can't reveal love because there is only one of them.[30] The multiple gods of other religions can't reveal love because they're always fighting. The everything-is-god religions don't believe in a personal god, nor do the "wisdom religions."[31] And for the materialist, "love is just a chemical condition of the brain."[32] Only the Christian God can champion love and relationship because only he is triune.

We have no human way to conceive of how God can be three in one. We may think of a team (many players, one cause), music (many notes, one chord) or water (liquid, steam and ice), but any analogy makes him less than three persons or less than one God. The mystery is essential, for the beauty of love is always indescribable. Rather than trying to explain him (which reduces God to the size of our imaginations), it is better to *marvel*. While we fight for clarity, God has no such concern. While we protect ourselves from others, his greatest joy is to be defined relationally. God does more than love: he *is* love for he *is* community—he is three distinct persons, yet without division.

---

[30] "Single-person gods, having spent eternity alone, are inevitably self-centered beings.... And if such gods do create, they always seem to do so out of an essential neediness or desire to *use* what they create merely for their own self-gratification." Michael Reeves, *Delighting in the Trinity* (Downers Grove: IVP, 2012), Loc. 559.

[31] Love exists in personal relationships, not abstractions.

[32] Timothy Keller, *King's Cross* (New York: Penguin, 2011), Loc. 245.

Triune Authority

Our exploration of the Trinity reveals the relational nature of God. Yet we must address a specific dimension of their relationship to fully understand their love, and that is *hierarchy*.

See how it is played out between the Father and Son:

> [Jesus], being in very nature God, did not consider equality with God something to be used to his own advantage; rather, he made himself nothing by taking the very nature of a servant… he humbled himself by becoming obedient to death—even death on a cross! (Philippians 2:6-8)

God the Father and God the Son are equal in every way, yet one leads and another obeys (John 5:19). How strange! Doesn't this contradict reciprocal love? Isn't hierarchy inherently oppressive and devaluing? So why does God choose to express his love through hierarchical relationships? It is because at the heart of loving relationships is *trust*, and the best way to express trust and trustworthiness is through submission and leadership. Love requires trust, and hierarchy makes trust indispensable.

We see how this works when we consider politicians. At what point did they have to be trustworthy and when did we have to trust them? It was when they assumed power over us. Trust is inseparable from power, meaning that trust is only necessary when power is present—and the more power, the greater the need for *us* to exercise trust, and for *them* to demonstrate trustworthiness.

If a person has nothing we want or need, if he has no way to harm or help us, there is no way to express trust. As awkward as this is, trust is only required when the possibility of ill treatment exists. This is why we avoid trust: we are trying to reduce the potential for hurt. We must see, though, that as mistrust seeks to lessen the power others have over us, it also lessens the degree of love and relationship in our lives (and the self-sufficient world that mistrust creates is just as damaging as any relationship can be).

Perhaps this is why we have mixed feelings about trust. We long to trust, but we avoid trust to avoid harm. For us, power equals possible pain. So we protect ourselves from others. The problem is that mistrust denies us the experience of intimacy. The barriers we construct to protect ourselves from pain also block out love. So we scratch our heads, wondering why we feel so disconnected and insecure, yet this is the natural result of living a self-protected life, a life that avoids trust.

We can treat relationships like clothes—they serve a function but are replaceable. When a relationship gets old or torn, we just swap it out for a new one. As a pastor, if I suggest that moving to a new church or city has the potential to tear the relational fabric of their lives, they look at me strangely. "It's not like I'm not going to make new friends elsewhere!"[33] Certainly, moving isn't always bad, but there is great cost in undervaluing covenant relationships.[34]

Treating relationships as commodities is not the only danger to relationships; so is the belief that rights and negotiation are the best ways to build relationships. This is often another way to avoid trust.

---

[33] The divorce rate in the US is 50% for first time marriages, 67% for second time marriages, and 74% for third time marriages, suggesting that moving on from relationship seldom builds relational health. http://64.233.161.104/search?q=cache:7kPsUi9Q2tUJ:www.christchurchepiscopal.com/Sermon_Archive/Newsleader/2003/Religion_Ethics_11june03.pdf+%2267+percent+of+second+and+74+percent+of+third+marriages+end+in+divorce+%22++Jennifer+Baker&hl=Esc

Jack Hayford says that redemption costs God more than creation (God created us with words, but redeemed us through the crucifixion), implying that it is always easier to start a new relationship than work through an old one. Yet redemption is the only way to build true and lasting reconciliation.

[34] God describes himself as the God of Abraham, Isaac and Jacob (Exodus 2:24; 3:15). He values a multigenerational, covenantal view of relationship.

Why? Trust and power are like a teeter-totter: the heavier the power of one person, the higher the trust of the other. So it is tempting to try to balance power and trust: "Since I want power and you want power, the best compromise is 50/50; that way I can give the least amount of trust, and have the highest amount of power possible." Fighting for personal rights is thinly disguised mistrust; it forgets that trust is the basis for all relational intimacy.

Healthy trust is not easy to understand, let alone live out, but Jesus stands in contrast to our suspicion and control. While we grasp for power, Jesus empties himself. While our relationships are disposable, while we demand rights, Jesus expresses absolute trust toward his father by exercising absolute submission. Is there anything more stunning? In turn, God the Father receives this gift as an opportunity to exalt his son (Philippians 2:9). Together, they engage in a relationship that can only be described as divine.

What makes the love within the Trinity so remarkable is that they refuse to self-protect. Our suspicion of being devalued or abused is not present in them because it is not necessary. Nor is a fear of control or manipulation. It is their delight to lead and it is their delight to submit. For them, hierarchy is an opportunity to experience a relationship of trust-filled love. What a radical idea! While we construct our lives to minimize the need for trust, they abandon themselves to one another. God is so remarkable that even in hierarchy, love is his only motivation.

God's Love Expressed

So how does God express this love toward *us?* This is a troubling question because many people look at their world, consider their lives, and reach the conclusion that while God might love sometimes, he has other motives. To respond, let's examine three ways in which God expresses his love toward us: mercy and justice, personal relationship, and Christ's death and resurrection.

Mercy and Justice

First, God rules the world according to two qualities: *mercy* and *justice*. Together, they comprise love, for justice defends victims and mercy loves criminals (Exodus 34:6-7; Zechariah 7:9). Both are critical. Justice ensures that the rights and needs of the impoverished are upheld. Mercy ensures that there is a way out of condemnation for the guilty. True love requires consequences *and* compassion, law *and* freedom, judgment *and* forgiveness.

The challenge of upholding mercy and justice is deciding which of the two to use at any given moment. Parents constantly struggle with this: is this a mercy moment or a justice moment? There have been times when one of my kids has complained about their sibling and I have been either unimpressed with their case or too tired to respond. However, soon afterward, I would watch them execute their own revenge—when I didn't uphold justice, they would. At other times I've been too demanding and I haven't given them enough mercy. It is then that they become disheartened, and the joy of relationship is drowned in rules. How do we know when to do which? The answer is more an art than a science.

The miracle of God is that he governs the world with the perfect blend of these two qualities. If he imposed more justice, we'd all be in jail awaiting the death penalty, for (as hard as it is for us to believe) our sin deserves a more potent and immediate response. If there were any more mercy in the world, our present chaos would become universal anarchy. God is leading the world through the tension of mercy and justice.

People are quick to criticize how God runs the world, but their alternatives either have too much justice or too much mercy.[35] Moreover, it should be noted that people who want more mercy are usually hoping to avoid moral accountability, and people who want more justice are usually self-righteous and want all the *bad* people to get what they deserve. Both groups are hardly neutral in their critique.

While the idea of mercy and justice is straightforward, we are still left with questions. Did God really command genocide in the Bible?[36] Does he inflict terminal cancer on a young mother, or hell upon a child who has never heard of Jesus? What about the woman who hates God because she was abused by a pastor? Where is God's mercy and justice in these places? *Two* answers are required.

The *first* answer might be disappointing: trust God. However, do not think this means we must ignore reality; it means that we must start from a position of trust, not suspicion. We should think, and think critically, but when we think that we are more loving than God, our pride blinds us. But when we start with trust, we perceive facts differently.

This is seen in how we tell a two-year-old that he must eat less candy. If we discuss delayed gratification, the cycle of addiction, the

---

[35] "You are God's critic, but do you have the answers?" Job 40:2 (NLT).

[36] This unique moment in Jewish history was not about ethnic cleansing; God wanted a people to have a place to live in relationship with him (Numbers 14:41-45; Deuteronomy 9:4-5). God gave the land to the Jews only after the Canaanites continually rejected his terms of peace (Genesis 15:16; Deuteronomy 20:10,16-18; Joshua 11:19; Hebrews 11:31). And when Israel rejected God, he ousted them also, confirming that God's concern was sin, not ethnicity (Leviticus 18:28). The violent and exaggerated language used to describe Israel's victories (which was common for that day, see Joshua 10:40-42) must be held in tension, both with what really happened (gradual eviction versus annihilation), and with God's love for all peoples (John 3:16). See Christopher J. H. Wright, *Old Testament Ethics for the People of God* (Downers Grove: IVP Academic, 2004), Loc.6162ff.

early onset of obesity, or how "sugar bugs" make cavities, will this convince him to change his ways? The blank look on his face will tell us no. His real need is to trust us.

Trust and humility take us places that suspicion cannot. This is why in the Bible, when God is directly asked about his role in human tragedy, he doesn't defend himself (Job 42:1-6; Luke 13:1-5; Romans 9:19-21). He is not nearly as concerned about explaining himself as we are. This is because trust comes *before* understanding. When we start with believing that God is love, reality is explained, but in an entirely different (and better) way. St. Augustine says it well: "Unless you believe, you will not understand."[37]

A friend reminded me of the parable of a man crying out to God for help as he falls off a cliff. But when he sees a branch that can break his fall, he tells God, "Never mind." There are often two ways to interpret reality: one that sees God as actively helpful; the other that believes in coincidence. Trust determines which we choose.

The *second* answer to the cause of human suffering is that we are responsible. It is easy to blame God for the negative effects of our sin, all the while congratulating ourselves for the positive effects of our goodness! Furthermore, we justify our charges against God by using natural disasters or sickness as evidence of his cruelty, yet the Bible tells us that even nature groans under the weight of our sin.[38] This does not mean that we get cancer because we sin; it means that our collective evil and rebellion against God physically damages our world and its inhabitants.

---

[37] Quoted in Tim Chester and Steve Timmis, *Total Church* (Wheaton: Crossway Books, 2008), 162.

[38] Romans 8:20-21; Isaiah 24:5; Hosea 4:1-3. The one who negatively impacted the earth is Adam particularly and humanity generally: "Creation was not party to Adam's failure but was drawn into it nonetheless." Dunn, J. D. G., Vol. 38, *A: Word Biblical Commentary: Romans 1-8*. (Dallas: Word, 2002), 471.

Dr. Rice Broocks says: "Is the creator of the car a cruel and thoughtless person because of the millions of people that have died in auto accidents?"[39] It doesn't make sense to blame God for how we misuse the good world he created.

The point is: God is not on trial; we are. God gave us this world to rule in his name, and social and environmental troubles are evidence of our failures (Psalm 8:4-6). Our blame shifting is further evidence of our unwillingness to take responsibility. If we are so caring, then let us prove it through humility and sacrifice. It is then that our eyes might adjust to see how far God's love and sacrifice surpasses ours.

Soon enough, heaven will come to earth in its fullness. Now, however, we live in the age of decision, which means that God allows wrongdoing to exist so that we can learn to hate sin and choose love. He designed the world with enough justice to feel the consequences of sin, and enough mercy to give us time to repent. So the question is not whether God is merciful and just; it is whether we will trust *his* mercy and justice over our own.

Personal Relationship

The first way that we see God's love is in the way that he rules the world with mercy and justice. The second way God shows his love is through desiring to have a personal relationship with us (Hebrews 8:11; Revelation 21:3-4). Some Christians believe that the chief end of man is to *glorify* God, but scripture plainly states that our highest purpose is to *love* God and others:

> Jesus replied: "'Love the Lord your God with all your heart and with all your soul and with all your mind.' This is the first and greatest commandment. And the second is like it: 'Love your

---

[39]   http://www.foxnews.com/opinion/2013/05/22/does-oklahoma-natural-disaster-prove-there-is-no-supernatural-god/?intcmp=trending

neighbor as yourself.' All the Law and the Prophets hang on these two commandments." (Matthew 22:37-40)

God repeatedly tells us to worship him above all else. However, he does so for our benefit, knowing how important it is for us to rightly order our affections. Moreover, as with any good father, he receives our honor and gratitude as an expression of love (Psalm 63:3). In eternity, when we read of creatures singing, "Holy, holy, holy" forever, think of a love song bursting from the lips of those who've seen his beauty and majesty (Revelation 4:8).[40] To know God is to join in that song, for no one compares to his goodness and greatness.[41]

When love is the umbrella under which glory rests, we see that God is not an egotistical hypocrite: asking us to embrace the way of love, while being personally motivated by another agenda. He is not a distant deity who needs to be worshipped. He is a good father who desires our trust (Matthew 6:9). Certainly God is King of all, but he was first a father:

> "Before he ever created, before he ever ruled the world, before anything else, this God was a Father loving his Son."[42]

This is how God seeks to relate to us. In the face of our less-than-ideal experience of family and fatherhood, God is a loving father whose motives and actions are trustworthy. J. I. Packer describes the importance of seeing God this way:

---

[40] To say that God is holy is to say that there is no one like him.

[41] "The word glory denotes sometimes what is internal." John Piper, *God's Passion for His Glory* (Illinois: Crossway Books, 1998), 222. Therefore, to glorify God is to reveal to the world the essence of who he is. There is no narcissism here, only vulnerability, for he longs to be known by his creation.

[42] Reeves, Loc. 239. "For if God is not a Father, if he has no Son and will have no children, then he must be lonely, distant and unapproachable." Loc.1680.

> "If you want to judge how well a person understands Christianity, find out how much he makes of the thought of being God's child, and having God as his Father. If this is not the thought that prompts and controls his worship and prayers, and his whole outlook on life, it means he does not understand Christianity very well at all."[43]

Christianity is the story of our heavenly father adopting us into his family, where we share in the "heavenly harmony" that is God.[44] What an incredible invitation! His greatest delight is to be the father we desperately need and have always longed for—a father who not only loves us deeply, but who also gives us family in which to thrive and belong.

The fatherhood of God affects me personally. My father was diagnosed with Multiple Sclerosis when I was six years old and died when I was sixteen. Consequently, we never spent any meaningful time together. So when I became a Christian at eleven, the greatest change was having a heavenly father. His strength, care, and guidance transformed my life. Sometimes I worry about people who have a great dad. I realize the flaw in my thinking but I'm afraid they might not see that they also need their father in heaven.

Christ's Death and Resurrection

The clearest demonstration of God's mercy and justice, the most powerful revelation of God's desire to have a relationship with us, is revealed in the death and resurrection of Jesus. No other god has died for our sins. No other god provided a way for us to live with him at his own expense. God paid the debt for our crimes so the barrier between him and us would be eternally removed.

---

[43] J. I. Packer, *Knowing God* (London: Hodder & Stoughton, 1973), 224.
[44] Reeves, Loc. 1589.

> But God demonstrates His own love toward us, in that while we were yet sinners, Christ died for us. (Romans 5:8)

So when God says he loves you, believe him. He died for you. At ultimate personal cost, he did all that was necessary for us to have a relationship with him. While he accepts our choices to separate from him, and while his love requires justice to be brought against the unrepentant, his greatest longing is to be with us… forever. If you find it hard to trust his heart, look at his actions. The cross is God's pledge of love to you.

Again, God stands in stark contrast to our self-preservation. His love compelled him to die that we might live. Christ's brutal and unjustified crucifixion silences anyone who speaks of God as uncaring or stoic. In his death, God brought together mercy and justice in one momentous act, by satisfying justice at his own expense. The result is the opportunity to have an eternal relationship with God that is based on *his* love, not *our* (insufficient) performance.

From a volatile global economy to an unstable home or job, for most of us, uncertainty is a way of life. So when we look at God, it may be hard to believe that he is trustworthy and that his acceptance or rejection of us is not about our performance. How challenging it is to consider that pure love exists… for us! But his grace, his abiding intimacy, and his self-sacrifice confirm that the author of your life's story is generous and kind.

Lord and Savior

So who is this triune God? He is Lord and Savior (2 Peter 3:18). He is Lord because he is unequalled power. He is Savior because he is pure love and made a way for us to be with him. If we do not see God as Lord and Savior, then we do not see God. God has not left us blind; he corrected our vision by incarnating himself in Jesus

Christ. In Christ, the goodness and greatness of God is revealed in bodily form.

Here is the issue: mistrust blinds us to God's power and love. It is not hard to build a case for portraying God as powerless and loveless, just as it is easier to be a revolutionary than a president, or a fan rather than a player. Trust, however, works with the same facts as mistrust, but reaches completely different conclusions.

I am embarrassed to tell you how many times I have collected evidence that *proves* why I should mistrust my wife, my friends… and my God. I stare intently at sex trafficking and God is nowhere to be found, until I hear stories of God stirring people's heart to reach the enslaved. I listen to people's string of bad luck and then watch them worship God with abandon because he's given them something better than easy circumstances.[45] I read of a God who was crucified at our hands and his reply is, "Father, forgive them, for they do not know what they are doing." (Luke 23:24). What enables us to find hope in the darkness? It is trust. Trust transforms. Trusting that God is all-loving and all-powerful is the only lens through which we can rightly see God and interpret this world.

So I ask, will you trust God to author your life story? Will you receive God as *your* father? The risk is hard to swallow on this side of the decision, but dissolves afterward. Not only is God *worthy* to be trusted, he *must* be trusted if we are ever to experience the goodness of his love and power. This is the invitation he offers you now.

---

[45] For example, Debbie and I met Nick Vujicic while staying at a retreat center in Cape Town. He has no arms and legs, but his joy was contagious. See him on YouTube.

Chapter Two Discussion Questions

a) Why is the question of who leads our lives our most critical question? How do we distract ourselves from evaluating the quality of our life's leader? What is the cost of having an inadequate life leader?

b) Give examples to support the statement "Who we believe God to be determines the way in which we follow him."

c) Why do we need God to be all-powerful? Why are fear and love not necessarily opposites? Why would fearing God make us fearless?

d) Why is love more than a feeling? Describe how motive precedes action in determining the goodness of an action.

e) Why can a Trinitarian God encapsulate love better than a single god, multiple gods, or a spiritual force? Why is hierarchy beneficial in embracing trust and trustworthiness? And why must we put limits on human power?

f) What happens when there is "too much" justice in a relationship? What happens when there is "too much" mercy in a relationship? Describe how justice and mercy are present in Christ's death and resurrection.

g) Is there anything that is preventing you from trusting Jesus to be your leader, to follow his storyline for your life? Will you receive God as your heavenly father?

Chapter Three
The Setting

Creation

So far, we have explored how God's story is a true story, and how the Author's motivation, not only for writing this story but also including us in it, is love. With this as a background, we can now turn attention to the story itself.

Nearly every story begins with laying out the setting. We can see how important context is to understanding a plot by considering the care a writer takes to present the back story of its main characters— we can't make sense of their actions without understanding their background. God is no different, so he begins his story by describing the creation of the world. That background explains the meaning of life, from which the details of *our* lives can be rightly understood.

So how would you answer the question, what is the meaning of life? Answers range from finding individual fulfillment to meeting family expectations, but pursuing personal success leaves us lonely, and trying to please others leaves us lost. Instead of trying to invent a purpose, it is better to ask our creator, for creators always have a specific purpose in mind (Ephesians 2:10). As a woodworker, I have never replied to the question, "What did you make?" with the answer, "Uhhh…"

Those who don't acknowledge a creator see no overarching purpose to our existence. As a result, they are left with having to invent their own meaning for life, like disproving God, beating a video game, or finding fault with others. Even noble causes fall short in their outcomes if they ignore God. The best one to define us is our creator, for every good author takes great care to shape each character for a specific purpose.

The book of Genesis tells us who God created us to be, against the backdrop of God's purpose for all of creation.[46] Ancient Middle East scholar John Walton states that Genesis One describes the creation of the world as God building a temple where he would dwell.[47] Typically, ancient temples were built on high places to symbolize that particular god's rule over its subjects, but, in Genesis, God lives where we live. This makes his temple—this world—a place of connection with us (Genesis 3:8). This reveals the relational motive of God as well as the sacredness of Earth, for it is where God chooses to dwell with us.

Specifically, the creation story describes God taking an uninhabitable cosmos and organizing it into a place where relationship can occur. In the first three days of creation, God creates the three main qualities that are necessary for relationship:

---

[46] The book of Genesis in the Bible presents God as the creator of purpose, not matter. He did create matter (Isaiah 45:18), but Genesis one focuses on the *why* and *who* of creation, not the scientific questions of *what* and *how*. "Cosmic creation in the ancient world was not viewed primarily as a process by which matter was brought into being, but as a process by which functions, roles, order, jurisdiction, organization and stability were established." John H. Walton, *The Lost World of Genesis One* (Downers Grove: InterVarsity Press, 2009), 53. (See also, p. 134). In other words, they were more concerned with *who* was in charge, than in how matter was created.

This implies that evolutionary science does not have to contradict the Bible, for it seeks to answer different questions. For a summary of the topic, read: http://biologos.org/uploads/projects/Keller_white_paper.pdf (2012).

[47] The seven days of creation correspond to the seven days of a temple inauguration. Ibid., 78-85.

time, space, and resources.[48] More than just the basis for life in a physical sense, these three qualities are the basis for relationship. In the subsequent three days, he created that which would govern or fill those elements.[49] So when God calls all these qualities "good" it means that they are able to fulfill the purpose for which they were created—namely, to promote and sustain relationship.[50]

I remember my first official date. I was so nervous, I wanted every detail to be perfect. So, first, I "created" a specific *time* for us to meet—I called her up and asked if we could go to dinner and a movie on Friday at 6:00 pm. Then I created *space*—before the date, I drove downtown and found a nice restaurant just a few blocks from the theater. I even made sure I knew where to park the car. Finally, I used my *resources* to feed and entertain us. While all three elements for relationship seemed to be in place, I must complete my "creation account" by telling you that the restaurant shut down a few days prior, and between that and my awkwardness, our date was less than inspiring.

Back to Genesis One: after God created time, space, and resources, he made us. We are the "date" for which he created the world. Listen to God's first description of us:

> Then God said, "Let us make mankind in our image, in our likeness, so that they may rule over the fish in the sea and the birds in the sky, over the livestock and all the wild animals, and over all the creatures that move along the ground." So God created

---

[48] Ibid., 56-59. Walton describes day three as God creating the basis for food, meaning the resources that we need to physically exist.

[49] Waltke describes the first three days of creation as "form" and the next three as "fill." Bruce K. Waltke, *An Old Testament Theology* (Grand Rapids: Zondervan, 2007), 185.

[50] "Good" means that it is able to accomplish its intended purpose, namely relationship. Iain Provan, Regent College, *BIBL 610, Genesis*, Week 2, 2008.

mankind in his own image, in the image of God he created them;
male and female he created them. (Genesis 1:26-27)

This first description of us is dripping with relational content. First, when God says, "Let us make mankind is our image" he describes humanity as the product of an *us*, instead of an *I*, which reveals that God's image is relational. To be made in God's image is to be made *from* relationship, and, therefore, *for* relationship.

This is expanded in the next phrase, where our responsibility is to *rule* over other living creatures. While governing might not look relational, it means that we are responsible for more than ourselves. While all the other creatures are only required to reproduce after their own kind, we are told to show concern for others, acting as God's representatives to the rest of creation.[51] To be truly human means to care for more than ourselves (evolutionary theories of competition do not correspond with our original design).

The next sentence goes even further into relationship, where humanity is described as diversity: male and female. Marriage reflects the nature of God by being two persons yet "one flesh." This is why the Hebrew word in Genesis 2:24 used to describe a husband and wife as *one* flesh, is the same word that describes God as being *one* in Deuteronomy 6:4. Marriage reflects God's relational nature.[52]

Then, when God finished his work, the Bible says he rested (Genesis 2:2). Does this mean he was tired and needed a break? *Rest* is a wonderful word: it means to enjoy what is made by using it for

---

[51] Ibid. "We are the one creature among all the creatures that is conscious that *everyone* has to eat." Leonard Hjalmarson, *No Home Like Place*, 2013, 34, Draft Ed.

[52] Before the fall of man, when Adam was in perfect harmony with God, God still described Adam as being *alone* (Genesis 2:18). So when God responded by creating Eve as a *suitable helper*, the *help* Eve gave Adam was to heal his loneliness. The primary help we are to give each other is relational, not functional.

its intended purpose.[53] We rest from building a chair by sitting on it. We rest from raising kids by enjoying them. In God's case, he rested from creating us by living with us.

This is a beautiful description of God's purpose for creation. His goal was not to create the world and then go on vacation; his goal was to be with us (Leviticus 26:12). Never do I build furniture so that I can put it in storage, or parent my children so that I can spend more time at work. Likewise, God's rest is to be with us, for that is why he worked. "[Rest] is more a matter of engagement without obstacles rather than disengagement without responsibilities."[54] God's rest is to enjoy us.

Similarly, *our* rest is to enjoy relationship with God and others. After all those dirty diapers and times spent disciplining our children, we need to play together. After working hard to provide for our family, we engage with them. There must be times when we stop working and start enjoying. This is why Christianity is described as rest—instead of striving to find God, we enjoy being with him (Hebrews 4:9-10).

The story is told of a high-powered CEO on vacation, walking along the beach one mid-morning, talking intently on his phone. After he finishes his business call, he notices a simple fisherman relaxing by his boat with his young son. He shouts to the fisherman, "Why are you not out fishing?" The reply: "I've already caught enough fish for the day." "Why don't you go and catch more fish?" "Then what?" "Then you can make more money." "Then what?" "Then you can buy more boats and employ more people and eventually have a large and successful business." "Then what?"

---

[53] John Walton, 76. God's rest is less about "ceasing" and more about taking up residence in what he made; namely, creation. John Walton, "Creation in Genesis 1:1-2:3 and the Ancient Near East." (Calvin Theological Journal 43, 2008), 60.
[54] *Lost World*, 73.

"Then you can relax on the beach and enjoy your family." To this the fisherman replied, "What do you think I'm doing today?" Our life purpose is to enjoy God and others—today.

Descartes distinguished humanity from the rest of creation by our ability to reason or self-reflect.[55] Looking at Genesis, perhaps it is truer that we are human because of our ability to relate—to truly love others irrespective of their usefulness to us.[56] The very nature of being human is to reflect God's relational nature. All that is unique about humanity—our ability to reason, to be moral, to be responsible, to have a spirit, to choose—reveals that we are designed for relationship with God and others.

Purpose

Since God made us for relationship, he measures our personal health *relationally*, not *individualistically*. This is the opposite of how we are conditioned to evaluate ourselves (or others). When someone asks us, "How are you?" we might say, "Good!" And how might we explain our answer? Maybe we'd say that we got a raise, lost some weight, or enjoyed the outdoors. We typically define *"good"* individualistically: "I like how the world is pleasing me today." An old TV commercial captures this self-centered definition of *good*:

---

[55] "I think, therefore I am."

Provan says that being made in God's image has more to do with being made for community than about personality, freewill, intelligence, etc. He goes on to say that relationship is also what we lost in the fall. "Did the fall destroy more about relationship than about the goodness of the context? Creation groans then, for these reasons, regarding our dysfunctional ways of relating to one another." Provan, Week 3.

[56] We might think that animals "love," but we must not mistake love for instinct. When a swan sees an egg beside her, she lovingly nudges the egg back under her body to keep it warm. When that egg is moved farther away, the mother crushes the egg with her beak, for she now thinks it is another swan's egg. What looks like nurture is really instinct.

"Have you ever noticed how special life can get when it's focused on you?"

A few years ago I asked a family friend to place the concrete for the house we were building. I hadn't seen him for a while, and when I asked him how he was doing, his response was, "Great!" He went on to tell me that he hadn't been this happy in years because he had finally broken up with his common-law partner. I didn't know how to respond. Congratulating him on his newfound narcissism felt awkward. Expressing sympathy didn't fit. What was clear, however, was that he defined "good" selfishly.

When we define our life purpose selfishly, self-love becomes our greatest ambition… as if self-love needs more of our attention! The real problem is not that we don't love ourselves; it is that we are infatuated with ourselves (Ephesians 5:29). Using self-esteem as our reason, we brag about saying "No" to others, having "me time," or defending our rights.[57] I especially cringe when people say that they're learning to forgive themselves—how can *accepting* our sin replace Christ's *payment* for sin? We simply repackage selfishness under the banner of self-love.

Even self-hatred is a form of self-love where we hate disappointing ourselves (if we truly hated ourselves, we'd like failing, just as we like our enemies to fail). Suicide also is an act of self-love for it requires disregarding loved ones, who always want us to live. Certainly self-destructive behaviors are just that, but the solution is not self-love. The solution to loving ourselves poorly is to find a better source of love.

---

[57] "The enthusiastic claims of the self-esteem movement range from fantasy to hogwash. The effects of self-esteem are small, limited, and not all good." Roy Baumeister (1996). Quoted by David G. Meyers, *Psychology 9th Edition* (New York: Worth Publishers, 2010), 588.

In contrast to selfishness, God defines "good" relationally. We are doing well when we are in right relationship with God, our family, friends, and world.[58] We are not doing well if we mistrust God, ignore our family, treat others as commodities, or ravage creation. It doesn't matter how we feel; how we are doing is observed in our relationship with others.

If loving relationships define our life purpose, what do healthy relationships look like? They are *reciprocal*, meaning they *give* and *receive* love.[59] Think of a relationship where all you ever do is give, give, give. How about a relationship where you only take, take, take? Is either healthy? Counselors describe a relationship as dysfunctional when love flows in only one direction. It is not healthy because it is not reciprocal.

This is especially true with God. If we only receive God's love, we are spoiled. If we only serve God, we are used. So whether it is with God or others, our goal is to engage in a cycle of receiving and giving.

This means that a healthy life is based on a rhythm of receiving and giving love. Sadly, it is common to divide our time, not between receiving and giving love, but between love and selfishness. Employees work for the weekends. Young mothers give 24/7 and then demand personal space. Children do their chores to get money. Men pay for drinks in the hope of sexual favors. The religious serve God to go to heaven. Whatever the scenario, we naturally balance love with selfishness—we give to get.

---

[58] This is what it means to be "righteous." "To be righteous or declared righteous is neither a juridical act nor an ontological transformation, but a state of being restored to right relationship with God because the alienating reality of sin has been set aside." Scott McKnight, J. B. Green (Ed.), *Dictionary of Jesus and the Gospels* (Justice, Righteousness) (Downers Grove, IL: InterVarsity Press, 1992) 411.

[59] Matthew 10:8; Philippians 4:15; 1 John 4:19. "Love cannot be pleasing if it is not also mutual [or reciprocal]." Richard of St. Victor, 376.

Not only do we deny ourselves the opportunity to receive blessings as a gift, our own giving to others is suspect. Employees just want their paycheck. Mothers demand me-time. Children aren't expected to love freely. It is as if to be happy, we need to be selfish. When we balance love with selfishness, a cloud of suspicion, self-protection, and insecurity blankets our lives.

A healthy life balances receiving with giving, not love with selfishness. Reciprocal love puts our whole life under the banner of love. Like inhaling and exhaling, our life is a rhythm of receiving and giving—"We love because he first loved us." (1 John 4:19).

In this way, employees find fulfillment in work and further fulfillment in rest. Mothers delight in serving their children and receive free time as a gift. Children are unconditionally loved and freely love their parents through obedience. Christians receive undeserved mercy and love God for *his* benefit. Reciprocal love revolutionizes relationships.

One of the ways I experienced this is in how I view mountain biking. I love the sport, and so over the years I've pushed to do it, justifying my demands with the belief that I deserve a little fun—a point of view that my wife grew to resent. Eventually, it became a huge point of tension in our marriage. I'm embarrassed to say how hard it was to give up my "right to ride," but I finally decided to hang up my helmet. After a few months, however, something amazing happened. One day my wife casually remarked, "You haven't gone riding for a while—you should go have some fun!" I felt like I'd been dipped in chocolate. The miracle, though, is not that I got to ride again. Biking shifted from being a personal right to an undeserved gift. Reciprocal love transforms everything.

Understanding that love is our life purpose redefines more than the word *good*. *Success* is redefined to describe those who love well, not those who are rich. *Happiness* is the byproduct of loving relationships, which is why it is so elusive for the self-absorbed. *Maturity* shifts from meaning independence to selflessness. *Self-control* is the ability to delay personal pleasure for the benefit of others.

Perfection must also be rethought, especially when we read that Jesus commands us to be more perfect, holy, and righteous than the religious elite of his day (Matthew 5:20, 48).[60] That seems impossible, not to mention exhausting! Only one thing exceeds legalistic perfection: love. To illustrate true perfection, look at the picture that my oldest son drew when he was little:

From this drawing, I look like a large man who might be choking his son, while my wife looks on in her see-through dress. Artistically and conceptually, there are some issues.

Now read the words he wrote to me. How do you think I feel about his picture? It is perfect.

---

[60] Righteousness is a relational quality: "The righteous are those who participate in and preserve a covenant relationship with God or other persons." Bromiley, G. W. (1988; 2002). *The International Standard Bible Encyclopedia, Revised.* Wm. B. Eerdmans.

God's only longing for us is to "draw" our lives with love. Others might criticize our attempts at love, or we might be disappointed with our performance, but God views us differently. He cares about our *direction*, not our *perfection*. As we live in response to his love, we are successful, mature, happy, holy, and… perfect.

Work

One of the main areas that love redefines is the area of work. For some, our jobs are a necessary evil, and for others they are our identity; neither is a healthy way to view work. To understand the true meaning of our work, we must understand *God's* work, for *our* work is meaningful to the degree that it imitates and continues *his* work. For what does he labor? We saw in Genesis One that God worked to create the time, space and resources for relationship to occur.

We carry on his work by understanding that what makes our effort meaningful is relationship. For instance, architects, engineers, and tradespeople create space for people to live and work together. Internet, phone, and paper companies help us communicate. Parents work to raise relationally healthy children. Plumbers create systems of waste removal so that we can live in community (a special "thank you" to plumbers). Food and health industries help us live and thrive (very helpful for relationship). Clothing companies decrease social embarrassment. Charities serve the needy. Governments bring order and peace. What noble activities these are! All labor is redeemed when it supports relationship. On the other hand, if our motives are selfish, our hard work is relationally meaningless and potentially idolatrous.

This means that what makes work meaningful is less about *what* we do, and mostly about *why* we do it. Thinking of my own employment history, I have been a groundskeeper, schoolteacher, paper mill worker, carpenter, janitor, and pastor, to name a few. Looking over these roles, I can tell you that I have resented and loved every one of them. What made the difference? It is not about *what* I did; it is about *why* I did it. When love is our main motive, it is then that our deeds are truly good.

Work gets meaningless when it is only about using our talents or filling our bank accounts. Maybe if we worked for relationship instead of self-fulfillment or personal benefit, we wouldn't resent the 40+ hours at the office or job site. Relationship redeems work.[61]

This does not mean that we shouldn't try to make money or maximize our skills; it means that we must first shift our motives. When love is our motive, our pursuit of success or excellence is to benefit *others*. This transforms these things as a means to bless others.

We can make our work about performance and reward (as if we are more deserving of blessing than the poor). The Bible, however, revolutionizes work by making it about giving and receiving love (1 Thessalonians 4:9-12). We work hard to serve God and others, and God loves us by graciously blessing the work of our hands (Deuteronomy 8:18). If we make work about getting what we deserve, we remain self-righteous and self-centered (Matthew 20:1-16). It is better to make work about exchanging gifts where we work to bless others and we trust God to bless us (Colossians 3:23-24). With this mindset, we become excellent employees because love takes us places that duty or self-fulfillment never can (Genesis 39:3; Daniel 1:20).

---

[61] The Bible describes even the purpose of money relationally (Luke 16:9). Craig M. Gay, *Cash Values* (Grand Rapids: Eerdmans Publishing: 2003), 95.

Needs

Not only does reciprocal love define our life purpose, it also explains our core needs. When we consider differences in culture, gender, age, or personality, it is difficult to even *find* a common set of needs, let alone *satisfy* them. However, when we believe that God created all of us in his image, we can see commonality in diversity.

Two relational needs that define us all are *security* and *significance*. God designed everyone to desire unconditional acceptance and meaningful purpose.[62] While the ways these needs are satisfied are as diverse as we are, we all want to connect and contribute.

How we choose our friends, career, or religion is by how well we think they will meet our needs. For as long as they give us a sense of love and purpose, we keep them. So when we treat our relationships, careers, and beliefs as fluid, this is a sign that we haven't found fulfillment in those places.

How do we meet our need for security and significance? Our need for security is best met when we *receive love*, and our need for significance is best met when we *give love*. This is why engaging in reciprocal relationships is fulfilling—they meet our deepest needs. While we are tempted to find security through retirement savings plans and significance through status, these are unsatisfying—they are non-relational answers to relational needs.

Ultimately, these needs are met in Jesus Christ. Only he can give us *eternal* security and *eternal* significance. We will expand on this in a few chapters, but our ultimate needs can only be met by an ultimate

[62] Verses that describe eternal security: Proverbs 19:22a (NIV, 1984); John 1:12; 3:16; 15:15; Romans 5:1; 8:1-3, 31, 35; 1 Corinthians 6:17,19, 20; 12, 27; 2 Corinthians 1:21; 5:21; Ephesians 1:1, 5; 2:18; Philippians 1:6; 3:20; Colossians 1:14; 2:20; 3:3; Hebrews 4:16; 1 Peter 1:3, 4; 1 John 4:17, 18; 5:18.

Verses that describe eternal significance: Jeremiah 1:5; Matthew 5:13, 14; John 15:1, 5, 16; Acts 1:8; Romans 8:28; 1 Corinthians 3:16; 12:7, 27; 2 Corinthians 5:18; 6:1; Ephesians 2:6, 10; 3:12; Philippians 1:6; 4:13; 2 Timothy 1:7, 9; 1 Peter 4:10.

source. As beautiful as a mother's love is, as intoxicating as romance or success can be, they can never fully satisfy us.

This implies that it is best to view others as *channels* through which God fulfills our needs. The acceptance we find in a spouse, or the meaning we find in a career need not compete with God; they are simply ways that Jesus mediates his love and meaning to us. The key is to distinguish *means* from *source*. When we mistake the means for the source, we become demanding and discouraged. However, when the source is clear, we can be grateful for our relationships or employment, however imperfect they may be.

In spite of the means, it is always true that security and significance are found in freely receiving and giving God's love (Matthew 10:8). Therefore, the more we demand or pursue satisfaction selfishly, the more disappointed we are. *We were made to share God's love.* Anything else leaves us unfulfilled.

Conclusion

If our life purpose is to give and receive God's love, and love is a motive, this leads us to a fascinating conclusion: our life *purpose* is really a life *motive*. Fulfillment is not found in *what* we do, but in *why* we do it. This means that changing diapers or caring for an elderly parent can have eternal importance, while using our talents or getting recognition can be empty, because the presence of *love* determines an action's ultimate value. This also means that we don't have to wait to graduate, get our dream job, find our soul mate, or have children before we feel fulfilled. Every moment of the day can be injected with eternal significance when love is our motive (1 Corinthians 13:13).

This helps explain why we might be disappointed with or uninterested in God. Maybe it is because our agenda is different than his. We want riches, success, and pleasure, but he offers love.

Following God might involve wealth or poverty, success or failure, pleasure or suffering, but when we see that love is his goal, his actions make sense; life becomes fulfilling regardless of our situation (Philippians 4:12). Understanding God's purpose for our lives helps us understand his actions and how he interacts with us.

I am often humbled by listening to people who have found God in the midst of a tragic situation. How can people who have lost so much, have so much peace and joy? They are motivated by a life purpose that considers even pain a privilege. This is true freedom: to be defined by someone greater than us or our circumstances.[63]

So, will you let God's love define you? Will you let it be the lens through which you understand God and his creation? Will you let it define your life purpose? Ultimately, the result is peace. This peace is not only the removal of war, it is the presence of "shalom"—an unhindered, pure, fulfilling, right-ordered relationship with the living God that sets every part of our lives and world in perfect harmony.[64]

As wonderful as this is, when we settle in our hearts that we want God's love to define us, we are left with a disturbing reality: we aren't able to live this way. This is what the next chapter addresses: what undermines our ability to live in God's love.

---

[63] Total freedom is impossible, for gaining one freedom requires losing another: choosing sexual promiscuity means losing the freedom to be a virgin. True freedom is not the ability to do *anything*; it is the freedom to live as God intended us to live. We are free, then, when we rightly love God and others without internal or external restraint.

[64] Hjalmarson, 44.

Chapter Three Discussion Questions

a) Why does having a creator imply purpose? Why does denying a creator undermine purpose?

b) How have you heard people describe the meaning of life? From Matthew 22:37-40, what is our life purpose? What happens to our life when something other than love and relationship is our ultimate life purpose?

c) If God defines our personal health according to the health of our relationship with God and others, on a scale of 1-10, how healthy are you? Why did you choose that number?

d) Why are "reciprocal" relationships particularly healthy?

e) Define goodness, success, happiness, maturity, and perfection from a love perspective. What makes work and play truly fulfilling?

f) How do people try to find security and significance outside of God? What happens if we try to make people, money, success, or pleasure our source of security or significance? Why is God a better source?

g) Is there anything stopping you from making love your life purpose?

Chapter Four
The Conflict

The Mark

Have you ever listened to someone tell a story that had no tension in it? It's boring! Telling us that you watched a movie with your spouse is not a great story because it lacks suspense. In contrast, if you told us that you had a big argument, but instead of stonewalling, you gave a card with an apology and two movie tickets, now we have a compelling story.

A good story needs conflict. In fact, the greater the tension and the harder the choices, the more compelling the story. As much as we dislike discomfort, challenges enable us to transcend mere existence. So what is the conflict in *God's* story?

So far, we have seen that the only way out of a selfish existence is to find and follow a relational God. The Christian God uniquely fits the role because he is triune—he is relationship within himself. We reflect his nature to the degree that we adopt love as our life motive. So what undermines our ability to receive and give love? Sin. Sin is the main source of conflict in our lives. This begs the question: what is sin?

For years I thought that God defined sin as anything he didn't like. It seemed like an arbitrary list of do's and don'ts—as if God listed all human behaviors on a cosmic whiteboard and drew a random line down the middle, entitling one side "Good" and other side "Bad."

Christians corrected me by explaining that sin meant "to miss the mark." Fine, but no one told me what the mark was! How can I change my life's trajectory when I don't know the destination? I tried to be good, hoping that I was hitting the magical mark, but life didn't fit neatly into a system of rules, and avoiding random behaviors didn't feel like success.

Next, some counselors told me that my main problem was not sin at all: it was pain. This made sense because pain is so painful, and I certainly didn't want to be hurt, any more than I wanted to hurt others. So I pursued this direction for a while until I realized that it led me into selfishness—avoiding pain prevented me from receiving and giving love.

It became clear to me that pain and happiness were symptoms, not roots. When I tried to avoid pain and achieve happiness as ends in themselves, I became more demanding and self-focused. This led me to find out what was at the root of misery, and it turned out to be *sin*. Emotional pain and unhappiness are the fruit of sin, as much as peace and joy are the fruit of love.

At this point, it started to make sense. I began to understand that the mark is love and relationship, and that sin is missing that mark. So a definition of sin became clear: *sin is whatever breaks relationship* (Isaiah 59:2). God's description of good and bad is not arbitrary at all. He calls whatever *breaks* relationship *sin*, and whatever *builds* relationship *love*.

This means that when we read all those laws in the Bible, God is telling us what breaks and builds relationship (Romans 13:9-10).[65]

---

[65] "God's obligations are instructions, like the ones we get in presents." They describe how to enjoy right relationships. Scot McKnight, *Community Called Atonement* (Nashville: Abingdon Press, 2007), Loc. 583.

He calls us to obey his laws, not to earn his love, but to help us rightly love him and others. This is so useful, especially when we consider how easily we deceive ourselves and redefine right and wrong to fit what we want. While laws can't capture all that love or sin is, they are road markers, guiding us toward love and right relationship. So when we turn from sin and walk the road of love, we are led into relational happiness.

This explains why the outcome of sin is hell, or eternal alienation from God (Romans 6:23). Sin is choosing to think and act in ways that separate us from God and others. Hell is filled with volunteers; it is not a random punishment for people whom God doesn't like, but rather the natural outcome of selfish choices. Hell starts now for everyone who rejects relationship with God and finds completion in the afterlife.[66]

No wonder God hates sin! Wickedness is not about being free or naughty; it destroys relationship, making intimacy with God and others impossible. Even if we feel justified in our choices, our self-proclaimed innocence doesn't change sin's impact. It is relationally devastating.

Self-Centeredness

Sin breaks relationship because, at its root, sin is *self-centeredness*; it makes us the center, demanding that our needs and wants be met, even at the expense of others. John Stott quotes William Temple's definition of sin:

---

[66] C.S. Lewis says, "I willingly believe that the damned are, in one sense, successful, rebels to the end; that the doors of hell are locked on the *inside.*" C.S. Lewis, *The Quotable Lewis* (Carol Stream: Tyndale 1989).
"There are only two kinds of people in the end: those who say to God, 'Thy will be done,' and those to whom God says in the end, 'Thy will be done.'" *Hell: Isn't the God of Christianity an Angry Judge?* Tim Keller, PreachingToday.com, 2010, 4.

> I am the centre of the world; where the horizon depends on where
> I stand… . Education may make my self-centeredness less
> disastrous by widening my horizon of interest; so far it is like
> climbing a tower, which widens the horizon for physical vision,
> while leaving me still the centre and standard of reference.[67]

When I first became a vocational pastor, we ran a Sunday evening church service. A young man who visited one night had just arrived in Vancouver and had no place to stay. His "Jesus is Lord" pen convinced us that he was a good guy, so Debbie and I invited him home with us. He stayed for about a week and then left town with a new girlfriend, my wife's purse, and our car. Call me judgmental, but after that, our relationship with him was never the same. His self-centeredness broke his relationship with us.

Adam Mabry of Aletheia church in Boston says, "Like a hundred glasses dropped from a table, each one cracks in a unique way." While there are an infinite number of ways that our fallen nature expresses itself, what pedophiles, thieves, gossipers and wild two-year-olds all have in common is that they act for the benefit of self. The next time you see a shocking crime on the news and think, "I'm not that bad," know that your latest lie or argument had the same motivation. Perhaps the only difference is that you've figured out more socially acceptable and personally beneficial ways to be self-consumed.

Additionally, before we defend ourselves by listing all we *haven't* done wrong, understand that sin includes what we *should* but *don't* do. In God's eyes, not helping the poor is as bad as sexual perversion (Amos 2:7), just as beating video game bosses is no replacement for fighting real injustice. It makes sense that one of the greatest signs of sinfulness is boredom. Maybe we wouldn't watch as much reality TV if we engaged in the drama of God's love story.

---

67 John R. W. Stott, *Basic Christianity* (Grand Rapids: Eerdmans, 1988), 78.

When we see how self-centeredness is the real crime, it causes us to rethink evil. Who is worse, the prostitute from a broken home or the executive who figured out how being good is a great way to be greedy? Is it the unbeliever who serves the poor or the Christian who does nothing? Certainly we're all sinners in need of mercy, but we must base our judgments on God's definition of good and bad.

Selfishness begins with wrongdoing, stretches to include passivity, but extends even further to include self-sufficiency. Sin is a decision, not just to withhold love from others, but also to reject God's love for us. Sins are attempts to get what we want without needing Jesus Christ. *Sin is meeting a legitimate need illegitimately.*[68]

Therefore, our ultimate crime is to live independently of our creator. While self-sufficiency might sound noble, not only is it unfulfilling, it leads to evil. Think of how we excuse our sin: "I need money, so I stole it." "I need sex, so I cheated on her." "I want success, so I lied." "I need to exercise, so you'll just have to wait." Behind every sin is the belief, "I will meet *my* needs how *I* want." Yes, God wants us to be personally responsible, but when that becomes prideful independence, we break relationship with him and others. In the end, every way *we* invent to be loved (secure) or important (significant) outside of Jesus leads to sin.

I fear that we deeply underestimate the depths of our selfishness and its effects. Although we defend our sin by explaining the legitimate needs behind our actions, we still abuse others. Although we excuse our sin by pointing out our goodness, four acts of charity do not cancel one act of murder. If we use a glue bottle with one hand and an axe with the other, the axe always wins. Our numbness reveals that we misjudge our need of God and the depravity of our sin.

---

[68] Matthew 4:1-11 records how the devil tempted Jesus. In each instance, we read how the devil offered to meet a legitimate need or desire in a way that forsook God.

Relational Theology

So far we have investigated the effects of our self-centeredness, how it closes the door on receiving and giving love, and how it is *the* source of conflict. We now need to explore the foundation upon which selfishness is built: self-rule. If sin was only selfish actions, then maybe we could improve ourselves (and God should appreciate our effort and overlook our failures). Or, if sin comes from sinful impulses, then God should change our nature so that we would act differently. As reasonable as these solutions sound, they only deal with symptoms, for sinful actions and desires stem from using our God-given free will to be self-ruling.

To explain this, imagine a good man—someone who works hard, helps his friends, and loves his family. All who know him respect him. In spite of his moral goodness, however, he has one flaw: he refuses to become a legal citizen of his country. For that reason alone, the government must deport him.

Is this unjust? Should the government overlook his rebellion? Is it right to expel good people solely because they won't submit to authority? Yes, it is. Social peace requires common allegiance. If governments tolerate defiance—regardless of a person's other good qualities—it will destroy the country. It's not about a government wanting control; it's about a person rebelling against the foundation of social peace.

Let's apply this to our relationship with God, who is a just and merciful king. Should he let good people into his kingdom because they want a nice place to live and raise their families? Absolutely not. They must agree to submit to the king; otherwise a seed of rebellion would be sown in the land, and what began with their relationship with God will eventually divide them from others also.

A common accusation against God is that he sends good people to hell. Now we see why. We do not go to hell because of poor performance. We go because we refuse to be in right relationship with the king of heaven (Matthew 7:22-23). It is (yet again) a relational issue. Access to God's kingdom requires rightly relating to its king. If we refuse to do so, we will be exiled to the land of rebellion: hell.

At the heart of sin, then, is self-rule. All sin can be traced back to being our own gods.[69] This is the ultimate idolatry, and is at the root of selfishness. This means that sin isn't necessarily about wanting to be *evil*; it is about wanting our own way. The problem is that when we want our own way, and other people want their own way, our kingdoms will clash. To imagine the carnage that results from personal orbits colliding, imagine two-year-olds fighting over the same toy. Our only freedom is to lay down our personal kingship and submit to the only king who can bring peace.

At this point, it is popular for people to question God's credentials to be their king, but we mustn't distract ourselves from the deeper issue: we struggle submitting to anyone who isn't us! It is important to know that God is trustworthy, but unless we first work through our rebellion, our critique of God is suspect.

Being our own gods is at the root of everything wrong, but I am sobered by how easily we befriend selfishness, as if it is somehow beneficial. Society only adds fuel to our fire when they use selfishness to motivate us. They create lotteries so we will give. They tell us not to do drugs because we will hurt ourselves. They encourage us to learn so we will make more money. They appeal to vanity to sell their products. In the end, we might help the poor, avoid drugs, earn a

---

[69] Adam and Eve chose to eat what God forbade because they gave into the temptation to be their own gods: "For God knows that when you eat from it your eyes will be opened, and you will be like God, knowing good and evil." (Genesis 3:5). The temptation was to redefine good and evil to suit their own desires.

degree, and look good, but we have fed a monster that will not be tamed.

Unfortunately, "religion" offers little help. Self-worship underlies all man-made religions, in spite of the morality they promote. Satanism is not the worship of Satan; it is the worship of self: "I am mine own redeemer."[70] The government-sanctioned church in communist China, called the *Three-self Patriotic Church*, uses "self" as propaganda.[71] Secularism seeks to remove religious expression, which doesn't remove worship; it just exalts humanity to god status. Buddhism contradicts itself by telling us to extinguish selfish desire through self-discipline.[72] Hinduism believes salvation comes through personal works, knowledge, and devotion.[73] New age religions pursue self-actualization.[74] Even in Islam, salvation comes through personal obedience to God.[75] And when family honor is our highest aim, success depends on our self-effort.

Beneath the different wrappings of religions, the same message is inside: you'll be rewarded for good behavior. When *our* goodness

---

[70] Quoted in *Hells Bells, The Dangers of Rock and Roll*. Reel to Real Ministries, 1989. See also Aleister Crowley: "Do what thou wilt is the whole of the law." "Satanists [do not] actually worship Satan… Satan is viewed as a symbol of all that humans should strive for: freedom from God, a rebellious spirit, relentless focus on self, and delight in the so-called evils of the world." James A. Beverly interviewing the high priest of the church of Satan, Peter H. Gilmore. *Faith Today*, May/June 2012, 45.

[71] This form of Christianity is built on three principles: self-governance, self-support (financial independence from foreigners), and self-propagation (indigenous missionary work). The government appeals to self to prevent exposure to outside Christianity. Brother Yun, *The Heavenly Man* (Manila: OMF Literature, 2003), 50.

[72] Josh McDowell and Don Stewart, *Handbook of Today's Religions* (San Bernardino: Here's Life Publishers, 1983), 307, 313.

[73] Ibid., 284, 290.

[74] M. Scott Peck, "The goal of spiritual growth is the attainment of Godhead by the conscious self… the individual is to become totally, wholly God."

[75] *Today's Religions*, 396. Allah's mercy does not mean that he paid for our sins; it means he reserves the right to choose whom he will; and we tilt the scales in our favor when we obey him, especially as martyrs.

is the means to Nirvana, Utopia, Heaven, Paradise, Honor, or Liberation, self is savior. Allah doesn't save us (in the sense that he pays for our sin); Buddha just handed out road maps; we must pay for Vishnu's help; and Atheism doesn't even pretend to offer love. In every case, our present and future blessings depend on our performance, making *us* the hero of our life story.

This makes religion and rebellion flip sides of the same coin. Religion exalts self through succeeding at external standards; rebellion exalts self by succeeding at internal standards. Ultimately, the differences are insignificant, for both make *self* the focus.

This means that we can choose from only two belief systems: the worship of self or the worship of Jesus. More will be said in the next chapter, but only Christianity bases relationship on mercy rather than good works, making it the only belief system that has love at its core.

With this understanding, hell makes perfect sense, in both its existence and its qualities. God created a place where self-worship finds full expression, and it ends up consuming its inhabitants. C.S. Lewis, in *The Great Divorce*, describes hell as a place where people can't get along with their neighbors, so they keep building houses farther and farther away from each other. When we are governed by self-rule, we start with feeling lonely and misunderstood, then eventually everyone becomes our enemy, and finally we experience relational death—eternal alienation from God. Our punishment is as much self-inflicted as it is applied by the hand of God (Isaiah 3:9).

At the root of all sin, then, is a rejection of God through the worship of self. When we resist his love and authority, we break relationship with him, for that is who he is.[76] And when we are

---

[76] Romans 1:21a describes our rejection of God's authority and love this way: "For although they knew God, they neither glorified him as God nor gave thanks to him." Our chief crime is not to acknowledge God's authority or thank him for his love.

estranged from him, we are soon alienated from others, for we have separated ourselves from the source of love. Therefore, the result of our freedom from God is present and eternal death.

Selfishness is the reason for everything wrong in us and this world. Self-worship has never been our friend and it never will be. The problem is that any attempt to free ourselves from its grip is just one more act of self-righteousness, which is what got us into this mess at the start! The only way to be free of selfishness is by receiving something from outside ourselves, something that has the power to deliver us from evil. That some*thing* is a some*one*: Jesus Christ.

This is the central conflict in God's story. It is not about whether we will be good or bad. It is whether we will deny the fleeting benefits of being our own gods and submit to the loving leadership of Jesus Christ. Deciding who will author our life story, then, is *the* decision that determines everything else.

Conclusion

The end of chapter four brings us to a fourth question: will you admit your sin? Twelve-step programs confirm that the beginning of finding a right solution is identifying the right problem.[77] If we think that the root issue is pain, a lack of education or opportunity, poor self-image, or negative circumstances, we will seek corresponding solutions. As bad as any of these issues are, there is one problem that undergirds all the rest, and that is our sin and rebellion against God. Unless we start here, any remedy we choose will be cosmetic.

Not only must we admit that sin is the root problem, we must also see how horrible it really is. If we describe our sin as mistakes, slip-ups, moments of weakness, genetic dispositions, or someone else's fault (God included), we will never change. As strange as it sounds, we won't grab hold of love until we fall into the depths of our depravity. This is the tension in God's story: we are not spectators in a theatre; we are the villains in a real-life drama. The tension is facing who we really are and admitting our need for salvation.

---

[77] Step One: "We admit we are powerless over our addiction—that our lives have become unmanageable."

So, will you admit your sin? Will you admit it is your core problem, and that it is willful, selfish, abusive, and divisive? Will you agree that your core crime is rebellion against your heavenly Father, and that a damaged relationship with him leads us to abuse every other relationship (demanding from others what only God can give)? If you admit you have a problem that you can't solve, you create room for God to save you, which is what the next chapter is about.

Chapter Four Discussion Questions

a) What did you grow up thinking it meant to be sinful or bad?

b) According to Isaiah 59:1-2, what breaks relationship?

c) Work backwards through the Ten Commandments, and describe how breaking them breaks relationship with God and others (Exodus 20:1-17).

d) Why are selfishness and love opposite motivations?

e) Why must God insist on having no competing rulers in his kingdom? When is independence evil? Describe how sins are our attempts at meeting our personal needs outside of God.

f) Are you sinful? How have you rebelled against God? What is the result of your sin and rebellion?

Chapter Five
The Hero

Saved Versus Helped

Thus far, we have seen that God is relational and we are made in his image. The problem is that our sin and self-rule separate us from God and others. Insecurity, confusion, aimlessness, pain, fear, abuse, powerlessness, or loneliness… these are all symptoms of our alienation from God.[78] In spite of its promises, all sin does is erode who God made us to be and his destiny for our lives. The question we need to answer here is: how can we be saved from sin?

If we think about how to get right with God, maybe we imagine doing what we do in other relationships: apologize and try harder. But before we consider any of our options, God must do something first: save us.

To explain this, picture yourself on the roof of your flooded home. The nearby river has overflowed its banks, leaving you stranded without supplies. We could examine your escape plan: wave your arms and scream for help, etc., but this is hardly the point. The real issue is that you need a rescuer to save you. This is how we need God's salvation.

There are at least two reasons why we can't save ourselves. The first reason is simple: we lack the ability. How can self save us from

---

[78] Erickson, 641, 645, 939.

self-centeredness? Even if we didn't want to be selfish anymore, not only do we lack the ability, every act of self-effort is another act of being our own lord and savior! To be saved from our sin and rebellion, we need outside help.

This leads us to the second reason. Picture yourself on the roof again. Let's say that you figured out how to build a raft from drifting debris and float your way to dry land. Your ingenuity "saved" you, but you weren't *loved*. Remember how we said that the goal determines the means. If the goal is love, then you must be rescued by someone other than you. Only then could you say, "I was loved." To be saved is to be loved in the deepest way possible.

So if the goal is to be saved from a loveless existence, *inability* is our first problem, but *ability* is our second problem, meaning that self-effort can't save us into love. Someone else must freely give us what we don't deserve but desperately need.[79] What is so remarkable about God's salvation is that it addresses both issues. First, God does what we *cannot* do for ourselves.[80] Second, God does what we *must not* do for ourselves. His provision is both a necessity and a gift, making it invaluable, compassionate salvation.[81]

---

[79] Just like we're not receiving love when we receive a paycheck, so it is with salvation. If we earn it, it isn't a gift of love; it is just payment for our effort (Romans 4:4).

[80] Our sin is not only behavioral, it is inherent (Romans 7:18). "Original sin is not an act but a broken relationship, and that is something that we have inherited." (Bray, 382). So we are "double sinners": born in sin and choosing it personally. Our sinful acts affirm our approval of Adam's original rebellion. Since sin is rooted in our very nature, we need more than education, self-effort, or positive thoughts to deliver us from its hold. In fact, any act of self-righteousness simply reinforces our pride and independence. Because we are born with a sin nature, freedom from sin requires a new nature, a nature we are unable to create or earn. This is what Jesus gives (Romans 5:6; Acts 4:12).

[81] Keller explains that we can make ourselves a Buddhist, Muslim, etc., but we can't make ourselves a Christian; it is a gift bestowed upon us—which is why salvation is described as a new birth (John 3:3). *The Gospel Coalition*, May 23, 2007.

Necessity + Gift = God's Salvation

It can be uncomfortable to need God! This is why we prefer to rely on ourselves; we like being masters of our destiny. This is also why we prefer God's *help* over God's *salvation*. If he just gave us advice or resources, we could retain control, but salvation puts us at the mercy of the giver. Pride and suspicion makes this hard for us.

Nevertheless, consider this: what if God designed us as dependent beings, not so that he could control us, but so that he could love us?[82] What if our total depravity enables us to experience total love? The depth to which we need him is the depth to which he can love us. Complete need equals complete love. This is why God wants to save us; he wants us to experience the depth of his love. Long to be saved and not just helped!

Who Is Jesus?

Once we see the need for salvation, how does God save us? Through Jesus Christ. We are not saved by an idea, a plan, or a power; we are saved by a *person*. In this way the means matches the end, for if the end is love, the means must be personal.

Who is this person, Jesus? Was he just a great moral teacher? Here is what C.S. Lewis says about that option:

> A man who was merely a man and said the sort of things Jesus said would not be a great moral teacher. He would either be a lunatic—on the level with the man who says he is a poached egg—or else he would be the Devil of Hell. You must make your choice. Either this man was, and is, the Son of God, or else a madman or something worse. You can shut him up for a fool, you can spit at him and kill him as a demon or you can fall at his feet and call him

---

http://m.youtube.com/#/watch?v=FfEnPeKUQcc&desktop_uri=%2Fwatch%3Fv%3DFfEnPeKUQcc

[82] "Creation is not a self-contained reality." Bray, 229.

Lord and God, but let us not come with any patronizing nonsense about his being a great human teacher.[83]

If Jesus is more than a good person, who is he? For him to save us, he must be 100% God and 100% man.[84] Every heresy about Christ tries to remove the paradox of Jesus being fully God and fully man, but this is who we need him to be.[85] Why must he be both? It is because Jesus *is* relationship, meaning that his very nature unites

---

[83] C.S. Lewis, *Mere Christianity* (HarperCollin e-books), 58.

[84] Psalm 110:1; Matthew 21:18; John 1:1-2; 4:6, 18; 5:18; 20:28; Romans 5:15; 9:5; Hebrews 1:3,8; 4:15. The historic description of Jesus is captured in the Council of Chalcedon (451 AD): "We confess one and the same Son, our Lord Jesus Christ, perfect in Godhead and also perfect in manhood; truly God and truly man, of a rational soul and body; consubstantial with the Father according to the Godhead, and consubstantial with us according to the Manhood; in all things like unto us, without sin; begotten before all ages of the Father according to the Godhead, and in these latter days, for us and for our salvation, born of the Virgin Mary; acknowledged in two natures, without confusion, without conversion, without severance, and without division; the distinction of natures being by no means taken away by the union, but rather the property of each nature being preserved, and concurring in one Person and one Subsistence, not parted or divided into two persons, but one and the same Son, and only begotten, God, the Word, the Lord Jesus Christ."
The virgin birth made possible the uniting of full deity with full humanity. It guarantees Christ's true humanity, yet without inherited guilt (Isaiah 7:14; Luke 1:34-35). Jesus had neither a sin nature nor did he practice sin (Hebrews 4:15). So his death on the cross was not for his own sins, but for ours (1 Peter 3:18).

[85] Common heresies: Jesus' humanity and divinity created an entirely new nature (Monophysite heresy); he was only a prophet (Ebonite heresy); he is the first and greatest of all created beings (Arianism); he was part human and part God (Apollinarianism); he was two persons in one body (Nestorianism); or he just appeared human (Doceticism). Dietrich Bonhoeffer, *Christ the Center* (San Francisco: Harper Collins, 1978 edition). See also H. Wayne House, *Zondervan Charts,* Chart 49, 2006.
Even secular writers at the time of Christ attest to Jesus' miraculous birth, life, miracles, death, and claimed resurrection. In Roman writing, see Tacitus (Annals 15.44) and Pliny the Younger (Letters 10.96). In Jewish writing, see Josephus (Antiquities 18.3.3). Michael Green and Gordon Carkner, *10 Myths about Christianity,* 50.

God and man. He reconciles us to God in his *person*, not just in his actions. No one claims to be God in the flesh (except those who think they are fairies that sprinkle the world with love dust), but Jesus did and is. He is unique for only in him are God and man perfectly united.

We must pause to consider how profound this is. Why would an eternal God choose to change his very nature to be with us? What kind of God does this? Nothing can adequately explain Christ's motives except love. I once heard author and pastor Ken Blue explain why Jesus healed on the Sabbath (an action that violated Jewish law). Was Jesus reinterpreting the law, resisting Jewish authority, or proving his power? A better explanation is that he couldn't let the man suffer another day. From healing a man, to dying on the cross, to changing his nature, there is nothing Jesus won't do to love us and his Father.

For this reason, the German theologian and martyr Dietrich Bonhoeffer summarized Christ's ministry as *pro me*.[86] Everything Jesus does is "for me," loving us in ways that are profoundly vital and personal. No other motive is lurking under the surface. Contrary to our complex and conflicted motivations, Jesus is love.

Reconciliation, then, is a word that perfectly captures *who* Jesus is, because not only are man and God united in his being, everything he did was to make a way for us to be in relationship with him (2 Corinthians 5:19). *How* does he reconcile us? He does this by being our Lord and Savior.

---

[86] Dietrich Bonhoeffer, *Christ the Center* (San Francisco: HarperCollins, 1978), 47. "For even the Son of Man did not come to be served, but to serve, and to give his life as a ransom for many." Mark 10:45.

Lord

What is a Christian? Is it someone who has invited Jesus into their heart? Is it someone who believes in God and the Bible? Are Christians those who go to church and try to be good people? We understand what a Christian is when we grasp God's overarching purpose. Matthew 6:10 summarizes it perfectly:

> Your kingdom come, your will be done, on earth as it is in heaven.

Christians obey the will of their King, Jesus (Matthew 7:21). This is the critical factor that determines whether love will win on earth. Without submission to a common king—love, peace, and joy are empty dreams. Following Jesus is good news because, as we've already discussed, our life and society is shaped primarily by who leads it.

> The ultimate issue in the universe is leadership. Who you follow and what directs your life is the single most important thing about you. Tell me who your leader is… and I can immediately tell all kinds of things about you… even if your leader is yourself, which is what most of us prefer.[87]

My professor, Jan Hettinga, goes on to say that we live in an age of "51-percent majorities, public opinion polls, and an increasingly distrustful populace," which makes following leaders a rarity.[88] We might attribute this to a lack of trustworthy leaders, but this reason cannot apply to Jesus, making any rebellion against him unjustified and inexcusable.

We must face the fact that submitting to Jesus is not an option (Philippians 2:10-11). God would be cruel if he did not insist on being king of the earth, for everything wrong and sick in our world can be traced back to us being our own selfish rulers. The question,

---

[87] Jan Hettinga, *Follow Me* (Colorado Springs: NavPress, 1996), 17.
[88] Ibid.

then, is not whether God will rule; it is whether you and I will submit to his leadership (Revelation 11:15-18). That decision determines whether we will be treated like citizens or enemies of his kingdom.

This diagram summarizes the challenge that faces us:

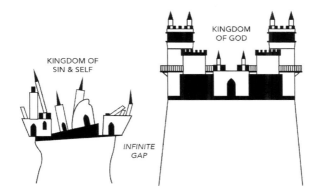

While there are many religions and beliefs, the Bible says that there are only two spiritual kingdoms: one is ruled by God, the other by sin and self. To establish a kingdom of love, God must ultimately destroy sin and self-rule. By deciding to follow Jesus, we are requesting a transfer of citizenship from *our* kingdom to *God's*. This is what it means to be a Christian.

> "Whoever wants to be my [Jesus'] disciple must deny themselves and take up their cross daily and follow me." (Luke 9:23)

So when we think of God's salvation, we must begin here. God saves us from self-rule by inviting us to submit to someone who is better and bigger than us. In this way, the movement in our relationship with God is not God fitting into our lives, but us entering into *his* life. Remember, God is about relationship. He liberates us from selfishness by transferring us into a kingdom, a society, a spiritual family, that rightly relates to him and to each other. This is our salvation.

This explains the importance of the first of the Ten Commandments: "You shall have no other gods before me" (Exodus 20:3). He says this, not for *his* ego, but for *our* salvation. If he is not the world's supreme ruler, the result is catastrophic. Not only would multiple leaders create division—no other leader is adequate for the job.

Imagine all the parts of a bicycle: handlebar, frame, chain, pedals, wheels, and so on. What enables them to be a bicycle? It is when they each agree to do their part, and their part only. If a chain decides to do a wheel's job, unity and functionality fall apart. This is what Karl Barth calls "a meaningful order of unity."[89] Whether it is a bicycle, a family, or the universe, each part of a system must do the role for which it was created if it is to work properly.

When it comes to our world and our lives functioning properly, Jesus must lead. If we vie for his job, we end up using people and things to compensate for our deficiencies—they become what the Bible calls "idols." We are idolatrous when we expect our spouse to complete us, alcohol to comfort us, careers to fulfill us, friends to amuse us, and knowledge to save us. We might think polytheistic religions are primitive, but "the first effect of not believing in God is to believe in anything."[90] The result is an addictive life that tries to replace our need for God with "more." This is why God commands our devotion. He is protecting us from idols that are ultimately destructive. When we pursue God above all else, the rest of our lives are rightly ordered.

---

[89] Karl Barth, *Church Dogmatics Vol.III:2* (Edinburgh: T & T Clark, 1957), para.46.1, 346.

[90] Emile Cammaert in, *The Laughing Prophets*, fictitiously quotes G. K. Chesterton. (1937) 211. http://answers.yahoo.com/question/index?qid=20091224050319AA640Dq

At the core of abuse is asking something or someone to do a job for which it or he or she was not designed—whether we use a hammer to cut wood or a lover to be our god. Money, career, talents, looks, family, friends, lovers, alcohol, virtues, or sex are abused by us to the degree that we look to them as our *source* of security and significance. None of these things are inherently wrong, but good things become bad when they're out of order.[91] No wonder we get disillusioned with them: they crumble under the weight of unreasonable expectations.

Therefore, the *order* of our relationships is as important as the relationships themselves. If I choose career over family, or family over God, all the relationships suffer simply because the order is wrong. To test this, prioritize your hobby over your marriage and see how that works for you.

It is common to contrast love and authority, but the most loving thing Jesus can do is rule our world and command us to worship him as Lord. This is the perfect solution to our relational dysfunction, for when Jesus takes his rightful place in our lives, we can live in harmony with him and others (Ephesians 4:16).

---

[91] See how people in various academic disciplines describe idolatry:

Theologian Millard Erickson says, "Sin is failure to let God be God and placing something or someone in God's rightful place of supremacy." (Erickson, 579).

Psychologist Larry Crabb says, "The primary problem with people today is misplaced dependency. We depend on everything but God to meet our fundamental needs." *Effective Biblical Counseling* (Grand Rapids: Zondervan, 1977), 139.

M.D. Gerald May describes addiction as trying "to fulfill our longing for God through objects of attachment." *Addictions and Grace* (San Francisco: Harper, 1988), 92.

Philosopher Søren Kierkegaard describes idolatry as building our identity on anything but God. Quoted by Tim Keller in *Hell: Isn't the God of Christianity an Angry Judge?* Christianity Today International, 2009, 7.

Pastor Tim Keller describes idolatry as making a good thing an ultimate thing. *Preaching the Gospel in a Post-Modern World*, 2002, 94.

Savior

Not only do we need Jesus to be our Lord, he must also be our Savior. What does it mean for Jesus to *save* us? Growing up, salvation meant that Jesus forgave my sins so I could go to heaven. While I appreciated being saved in the future, I had no idea how Jesus saved me daily. The result was a life that had much addiction, pride, and insecurity, but little of the peace and joy God promised.

I was so dissatisfied that I wrote my Master's thesis on following Christ in the hope that salvation would make more sense. I enjoyed my studies, but my discontent remained. Even after I became a vocational pastor, the only practical advice I gave people was to try harder—not the good news that a Christian minister should bring! I wrapped my advice in Bible verses, psychology, and optimism, but all I offered people was more to fail at (Luke 11:46).

I remember when the gospel finally made sense, when salvation went from a future hope to also being a present reality. Life didn't get easier after that, but life's journey switched from *searching* for God (and his blessings) to *walking* with God. This is the what we *all* need—not instruction manuals, warm wishes, or future promises. We need a connection with God in our present reality.

This is pivotal, for when we are rightly connected to God, then his love and power can transform our lives. Even though everyone feels good and acts good now and then, if we are unplugged from God, we are cut off from the source of life. Salvation, then, can be described best as reconciliation to God; and when we are in right relationship with God, we can experience life as he intends.

When this is the goal, Jesus is the only way, for he gives the two gifts we need to be reconciled to God. Acts 2 summarizes the Christian message:

"Repent and be baptized, every one of you, in the name of Jesus
Christ for the forgiveness of your sins. And you will receive the
gift of the Holy Spirit." (Acts 2:38)

Remember how we said that any healthy relationship requires
receiving and giving love? Well, Jesus' two gifts match the two sides
of relationship: we *receive* love in the form of his forgiveness (mercy),
and we *give* love through the power of the Holy Spirit (grace).

These two gifts transfer us from the kingdom of sin and self into
right relationship with God; not just in the future, but now!

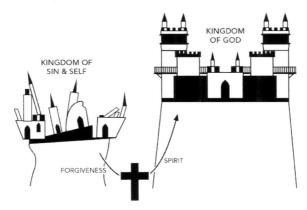

Let's explore the significance of these gifts further by looking at
God's mercy and grace.

God's Mercy

To be reconciled to God means to be at peace with him. How
is that achieved? Unfortunately, two common views of peace with
God (or others) miss the mark. The first imagines peace as a *feeling*,
where we try to feel harmony through things like meditation, sex, or
tolerance.

When I speak on campuses about love, sex and relationships, I try to have the event organizers survey students on the topic before I arrive. Typically, the survey results say that premarital sex and living together "feels right." Students are shocked to hear a study that found the divorce rate for those who lived together before marriage to be 80 percent higher than for those who didn't;[92] and one study reports that the divorce rate for those who were married as virgins is 3 percent.[93] What *feels* good does not always bring relational peace or harmony.

The problem with making peace a feeling is that it does not deal with reality. Extramarital sex might feel good, but the relationship is still harmed. Meditation might shift our focus onto something positive, but it does not solve what's negative. Medication might lift or lower our emotions, but our reality hasn't changed. Even feeling good about our relationship with God doesn't mean it *is* good. We might be able to distract ourselves with life's pleasures, but our guilt before God is *fact*, not just a feeling. It is sobering to realize that society is becoming increasingly content with a feeling instead of a reality. This erodes our ability to see our need for God—"Why should I follow Jesus when I can find ways to feel good without him?"

The second way to pursue peace deals with reality head on. Instead of *feeling* peace, we try to *make* peace. Here, we confront social injustice, improve our parenting skills, attack rebel forces, or strengthen our spiritual disciplines. We think that better rules or rule-enforcement produce peace.

---

[92] John D. Cunningham and John K. Antill, "Cohabitation and Marriage: Retrospective and Predictive Comparisons," Journal of Social and Personal Relationships 11 (1994), 77-93.

[93] Beverly J. Hadland, *Hang onto your Hormones* (Toronto: Life Cycle Books, 1992), 4, 91, 160-169. This statistic includes virgins and "secondary virgins" – people who were sexually active but then re-committed to chastity.

We can do this in our relationship with God. Religions are attempts to achieve a level of performance that *makes* God accept or bless us. We hear this attitude in how people pray: "Dear God, he really is a good person, so if you would just…" This attitude is horrible, for if our relationship with God is based on *our* performance, it is no longer based on *his* faithful love. This undermines security at its core.

Reality proves that no set of rules or level of performance can sustain peace with God or others. Historians speak of the vain attempts to negotiate with Hitler. Parents describe equally vain negotiations with toddlers. Corporations find loopholes in the law. Christians quickly turn relationship into religion. Addicts lament the power of their bondage. Sadly, effort, laws, or skills can never reach a level that guarantees lasting peace. In the end, *making* peace is as superficial as *feeling* peace.[94]

What is God's response to the persistence of disharmony? How can we experience eternal love and security? It is through mercy. By basing our relationship with him on *his* forgiveness, rather than *our* feelings or effort, our relationship with him is secure. This, in turn, provides a stable platform from which we can engage in less stable relationships.

What is Jesus' mercy? It is a forgiveness that blots out our offenses.[95] It is a reconciliation that removes the barriers between he and us (Ephesians 2:14-22). It is an unconditional love that gives us

---

[94] Just the rise of antidepressant use among children exposes the fact that our new techniques and abilities are not enough to quiet the turmoil in our souls. *Rising Prevalence of Antidepressants Among US Youths*, Journal of the America Academy of Pediatrics, May 2012, http://pediatrics.aappublications.org/content/109/5/721. abstract?ijkey=632739991db5df7f8aa85574a1f6558899729ee3&keytype2=tf_ipsecsha.

[95] Fausset's Bible Dictionary, "mercy" Biblesoft, 1998. "Mercy is God's pardon of offenders." Geoffrey W. Bromiley Gen. Ed., *International Standard Bible Encyclopedia* (Grand Rapids: Eerdmans, 1986), "Mercy."

the opposite of what we deserve. Mercy makes us eternally secure, for if we *earned* peace with God, our relationship with him would be only as secure as our latest effort. Instead, the gift of pardon ensures that even our sin won't separate us from God. It changes the basis of our relationship with God from *our* performance to *God's* enduring mercy. *This* is eternal security!

Mercy is not a casual dismissal of our sin, or an emotional response of pity. The substitutionary sacrifice of Jesus paid the penalty for our sin.[96] In his death, mercy and justice unite, for *mercy is justice paid at Christ's expense* (Hebrews 9:22). This makes us doubly secure, because forgiveness is both undeserved and just.

To explain how true forgiveness is an act of justice, imagine getting pulled over by the police for speeding (I can). If the officer lets you go without having to pay the fine, would you have been forgiven? No! You are still guilty—if the officer ever changed his mind, you could still be charged. For the officer to truly forgive your debt, he must pay for your ticket at his own expense. True forgiveness requires justice to be served.

This is what it legally means to have a debt forgiven. It doesn't mean no one pays; it means *someone else* pays instead of you. Without this payment, forgiveness is stripped of its justice, making it cheap and unjust. Christ's payment for our crimes, on the other hand, is neither cheap nor unjust.

A court scene captures what Jesus' forgiveness is. You are found guilty of a horrific crime in heaven's court, but—just as the Judge sentences you to death—Jesus steps forward and whispers something to him. The Judge listens intently, nods, and then says,

---

[96] Mercy triumphs over judgment. (James 2:13). Erickson, 818. "Propitiation" better captures the work of Christ than "atonement." The latter describes covering sin (as seen in Old Testament animal sacrifices), but the former describes Christ's work as blotting out sin completely (Romans 3:25; 1 John 4:10 NASB).

"This innocent man has volunteered to die in your place. Justice will be served by his death so I have granted his request. If you accept his sacrifice, his life will replace your own, and you will be acquitted." At the heart of salvation is Christ's offer to exchange his life for ours.[97] His substitutionary sacrifice deals with that *fact* of our guilt, which makes any *feeling* of guilt or rejection unfounded.

What is our crime that deserves death? Not only is it the accumulation of sins against others, it is treason against God. Our self-rule opposes God's rule; so unless we die, his kingdom of peace and joy cannot be established. Our rebellion cannot be tolerated, for it undermines any hope of God building a unified, peace-filled kingdom.

The only way to enter God's kingdom is to be acquitted of our rebellion, and only Jesus can do this. Because he was sinless, Jesus died for *our* sins instead of his own. As a man, he can die in our place; as God, his death has infinite value, sufficient to pay for us all.

Through Jesus, we have an eternally secure relationship with God because it is based on *his* mercy rather than *our* works. While other religions lay out a payment plan for good karma, Jesus pays for us to enter his kingdom at his own expense. Shocking! What kind of God does this? The mystery of Christ is not that his love is hard to understand; it is hard to believe.

The Bible story of the woman caught in adultery illustrates Jesus' love and its transforming power (John 8:1-12). Religious leaders brought the woman to Jesus, reminded him that the law required her to be stoned to death, and asked what *he* would do. Calmly, he invited

---

[97] "Atonement language includes several evocative metaphors: there is a sacrificial metaphor (offering), and a legal metaphor (justification), and an interpersonal metaphor (reconciliation), and a commercial metaphor (redemption), and a military metaphor (ransom).... [What they are all about is] God identifying with us so that we might participate in God." McKnight, Loc. 879.

anyone without sin to throw the first stone. Eventually, humility overrode judgment, and no one stayed to accuse her. With the crowd dispersed, this woman stood alone before her God and judge. But instead of facing the sting of condemnation, she met mercy face to face. That love released her to live in a way that the oppression of guilt had made impossible.

It is easy to underestimate the destructive nature of guilt, probably because we're often unaware of its presence. If we've not experienced God's unconditional love, a cold life of self-protection might seem as normal to us as swamp water does to a tadpole. But we can have a new normal. Jesus came to cleanse, refresh, and heal us, transforming how we relate to him and others.

Recently, I talked to a counselor who explained that when abusers do not find forgiveness, not only will they likely reoffend, they will also express rage. Her statement helped me understand someone I was reaching out to, but it also reminded me of how angry I had been as a teen. I assumed that my feelings were about my circumstances, and not about my own bondage to sin. But maybe my swings between rage and despair were rooted in seeing no way out of my guilt. This led me to consider the source of violence, depression, anxiety, perversion, and cold-heartedness in our society. What if these social ills are, at least in part, driven by the fact that we are all guilty before *God*? What if our spiral of destructive thoughts, feelings, and actions is rooted in a fact that is not fixed by trying to be more positive? What if our rebellion against God affects us more than we realize?

This is true for me. The way I dealt with my shameful past was to befriend darkness. I was terrified of being known, and so I lived an increasingly guarded existence. But as I risked revealing my dark side to others, they mediated God's mercy to me, and God's light became a source of warmth instead of judgment (1 John 1:9). While the fear of exposure described in John 3:17-20 is familiar to me, so is the salvation that comes through transparency:

> For God did not send his Son into the world to condemn the world, but to save the world through him. Whoever believes in him is not condemned, but whoever does not believe stands condemned already because they have not believed in the name of God's one and only Son. This is the verdict: Light has come into the world, but people loved darkness instead of light because their deeds were evil. Everyone who does evil hates the light, and will not come into the light for fear that their deeds will be exposed.

Jesus' payment for our sin does not merely gain us entrance into heaven. This mercy-based relationship changes the core of who we are. No longer do we engage with the world form a position of guilt: angry, fearful, and hard. As he cleanses, heals and softens our hearts with his presence (Ezekiel 36:26), we now view ourselves and others from a position of being known and loved by the King of Heaven. How profound it is that "there is now no condemnation for those who are in Christ Jesus" (Romans 8:1)!

Without mercy, life is nothing more than a never-ending pursuit to *earn* an acceptance that can only be *received*. With mercy, we not only *receive* love, we gain an opportunity to *give* love. Since our good works are no longer applied to paying off our debt (Jesus has already paid our debt), they can now be carried out purely for the benefit of another.

A while ago, Debbie and I lent a woman some money. Months later she told us, "I want to give you a financial gift. This isn't to pay down my debt; I just want to love you guys." Regardless of how she felt, her outstanding debt made gift-giving impossible. The same is true with God. Only if our debt is paid can our good works be truly for the sake of another. Mercy creates an opportunity for us to love others.

I must highlight this because we could see mercy as a way to be selfish, as in: "Forgiveness is my ticket to do what I want!" Yet God's intent for forgiveness is to enable us to *pursue* love, not *avoid* it. God says he forgives only those who forgive others (Matthew 6:14). This does not mean we earn forgiveness; it means that God forgives those who are motivated by love, not selfishness. God is committed to making love the currency of his kingdom. This is why having a mercy-based relationship with him is so critical; it is the foundation upon which we receive *and* give true love.

When I was in college, friends often borrowed my car. On one occasion, a friend hit a curb, bending two rims and popping two tires. He quickly apologized and offered to replace the two tires. When I went to the tire store, the salesperson explained that two new tires would upset the car's handling because the other tires were worn. So he looked up the price of the existing tires, and suggested I buy four cheaper tires for the same price. Being a broke student, I followed his advice.

A few days later, this friend approached me and said that I had ripped him off. He researched the cost of the new tires, and said he paid me twice as much as two of them were worth. I couldn't believe it! I explained what happened, but he kept on demanding his money back, so I decided to comply. In the end, the new tires were horrible, the rims stayed bent, and I was out half the money owed me. But mercy (paying his debt) gave me one thing: a restored relationship with my friend. That was worth more than the price I paid.

When Jesus' mercy invades the messiness of our lives, our hearts are changed and our priorities rearranged in ways that enable us to love as he loved us. In this way, his mercy leads us into a life of freedom and reconciliation.

God's mercy, then, is better than pursuing a feeling. It is a *fact* to act upon instead of a *feeling* to invent. Think of it this way: what is the best way for people to know if they're wealthy? They don't wait for a feeling; they read their bank statement! So when you feel condemned, don't try to *feel* forgiven; trust in Jesus' death and resurrection, and good feelings will surely follow.[98]

Think of the amount of time we spend manipulating acceptance, either from God or others. Consider the amount of energy we put into being defensive or hurting others before they hurt us. Jesus saves us so much time and energy! This is all because his mercy frees us from guilt. While we won't fully realize this before heaven, God shifts our life foundation from being guilt-based to mercy-based. We will still feel bad when we do wrong, but we can deal with sin in others or ourselves from a position of being *in* Christ, known and loved, instead of *outside* Christ, rejected and condemned. In this way, mercy saves us—every day! It saves us from insecurity, anger, fear, pride, condemnation, and alienation.[99]

"Mercy sums up God's saving acts and plan of salvation."[100] Through Christ's death and resurrection, we receive a free gift, a cancelled debt, an unconditional pardon, a complete adoption, a new birth, a new citizenship, an eternal security, and a new life purpose. This is the life that exists on the other side of Christ's death.[101]

---

[98] Keller emphasizes that the Christian message is good *news* versus good *advice*. Good advice tells us what we should do; good news tells us what Christ has already done. *The Gospel Coalition*, May 23, 2007. http://m.youtube.com/#/watch?v=FfEnPeKUQcc&desktop_uri=%2Fwatch%3Fv%3DFfEnPeKUQcc

[99] "Christ nullified Satan's control over us at the root—the power to bring us under the curse and condemnation of the law." Erickson, 839.

[100] Colin Brown Gen. Ed., *Dictionary of New Testament Theology Vol. 2* (Grand Rapids: Zondervan, 1986), 598. See also 2 Peter 1:3-4.

[101] 1 Corinthians 15:13-17, Grudem, 614. Given the critical nature of the resurrection, it stands as one of the most fiercely challenged historical events. Christ's resurrection is verified by these facts: a) Jesus' own followers had to be convinced of His resurrection, therefore they had no thought of foul play; b) Christ's enemies also did not want the resurrection or anything else to happen to

God's Grace

As incredible as mercy is, it explains only half our salvation. If mercy were all that Christ gave us, we would make it through the door of his kingdom, but no farther. Living in God's kingdom requires more than the removal of sin; we also need the ability to love God and others.[102]

This is where the gift of God's grace takes center stage. *Grace is the gift of God's empowering presence.*[103] It is unmerited favor and more. It enables us to live the life God intends for us.

> For it is by grace you have been saved, through faith—and this not from yourselves, it is the gift of God—not by works, so that no one can boast. For we are God's workmanship, created in Christ Jesus to do good works, which God prepared in advance for us to do. (Ephesians 2:8-10)

The gift of grace enables us to do good works, to fulfill God's purposes for our lives. Notice, then, that grace does not *remove* our responsibility; it empowers us to succeed.

> And God is able to make all grace abound to you, so that always having all sufficiency in everything, you may have an abundance for every good deed." (2 Corinthians 9:8) NASB

For years I was taught that mercy and grace were synonymous, that they both described God's forgiveness. With this definition, my relationship with God started as a gift, but continued through self-effort. No wonder I was so tired and unfruitful! Thankfully, I learned that God fulfills both sides of relationship—both the receiving *and*

Christ's body; c) Hundreds of eyewitnesses confirm the authenticity of the resurrected Christ.

[102] Mercy gives us the *potential* to love others, but not the *power*.

[103] Gordon Fee, *Empowering Presence* (Peabody: Hendrickson Publishers, 1994), 33, 86, 339, 498, 607, 840. Fee defines spiritual gifts as "concrete expressions of grace." 33.

the giving of God's love. He gives us mercy *and* grace; a gift of unconditional love *and* an empowering to love others.

The difficulty I had with my old definition of grace was not that it was incorrect; it just didn't go far enough. How sad to be saved from what's wrong but be given no power to do what's right! If this is salvation, then heaven is a group of sinners apologizing for eternity—"Oh, I'm sorry." "No, *I'm* sorry." Grace, however, changes our nature, transforms our heart, and infuses our actions with effective love (Ezekiel 36:26-27).

Do not think, however, that God's grace is something we possess, like a superhero's special powers. God's grace indwells us in the person of his Spirit.

> His divine power has given us everything we need for life and godliness. (2 Peter 1:3)

What does his empowering presence enable us to do? First, he transforms our *character*.

> But the fruit of the Spirit is love, joy, peace, patience, kindness, goodness, faithfulness, gentleness and self-control. (Galatians 5:22-23)

I love how a fruit tree bears its produce. It does not grunt and push and squeeze out a single fruit; and do it all over again for the next fruit. As the branches stay connected to the tree, an abundant harvest is naturally produced. So it is with us:

> "I [Jesus] am the vine, you are the branches; he who abides in Me and I in him, he bears much fruit, for apart from Me you can do nothing." (John 15:5 NASB)

"Abide" is a wonderful word that describes a restful, enduring connection to Jesus. As we rest in God instead of react to our surroundings, we naturally experience love, joy, peace, and so on. So, we don't grunt and push and squeeze out an act of love, we stay connected to the *source* of love. We are saved from words and actions born of self-centeredness and anxiety, simply by resting and walking in God's grace (Galatians 5.16).

God's empowering presence also transforms our *ability*. Grace is like a prism that refracts God's presence in our lives into a rainbow of supernatural ability, ranging from healing to serving, prophecy to wisdom—whatever is needed to practically bless others.[104]

> Now to each one the manifestation of the Spirit is given for the common good. To one there is given through the Spirit the message of wisdom, to another the message of knowledge... to another faith... to another gifts of healing by that one Spirit, to another miraculous powers, to another prophecy, to another distinguishing between spirits, to another speaking in different kinds of tongues, and to still another the interpretation of tongues. (1 Corinthians 12:7-10)

God fills *our* good works with *his* empowering presence, converting our love from mere sentiment, to effective help.[105] All our goodness is from God, yet all our hard work matters:[106]

---

[104] 1 Corinthians 12:8-11; Romans 12:3-8. Michael Griffiths, *Serving Grace* (Berkshire: Cox and Wyman, 1986), 18. The Greek word for grace is "charis," and for the gifts of God's Spirit it is "charismata," which tells us that grace manifests itself in supernatural gifts, tangibly revealing God's love and power. Donald Gee describes spiritual gifts as phanerosis, "a shining forth" of the Spirit, meaning that spiritual gifts are designed to tangibly manifest God's glory. Donald Gee, *Spiritual Gifts in the Work of the Ministry Today* (Springfield: Gospel Publishing House, 1963), p. 10. "Grace shapes itself to individuals and situations so that through them, God can work His purposes." John Koenig, *Charismata: God's Gifts for God's People* (Philadelphia: Westminster Press, 1978), 64.

[105] 2 Corinthians 3:18. Just like we can say of Christ's actions, "There is God!" and in the same moment say, "There is man!", the same can be said of us as we follow Christ.

[106] Romans 8:29. Dr. Klaus Bockmuehl described the Christian life as 100% God's work and 100% our effort.

> But by the grace of God I am what I am, and His grace to me was not without effect. No, I worked harder than all of them—yet not I, but the grace of God that was with me. (2 Corinthians 15:10)

What we see in this passage is a wonderful, inseparable blend of our effort and God's grace working in harmony. Some Christians are paranoid about work, believing that somehow work and grace are opposites. Indeed, we can't earn love, but the work described here is about loving others, not about securing God's acceptance of us. We can't work for the gift of forgiveness, but we can and must work to love others. And what hard work it is! God does not give us his grace to make us lazy; it is designed to strengthen our calloused hands with divine power. This means that if we don't work, we don't experience the work of his Spirit, for God can't strengthen what doesn't exist.

It is encouraging to know that God empowers our activity. Whether we are praying, parenting, or plumbing, God is fully present, filling our actions with supernatural power, transforming our words and actions into displays of his love and power (Acts 1:8). Talk about a significant life!

A few weeks ago, one of our sons was unhappy for an unusually long time. We did whatever we could to lighten his spirit, but he wouldn't even smile. Then, during one of our talks, I asked God to give him a picture of what was going on, and he saw himself as a ship that was plotting his own course instead of trusting in the lighthouse (God). When I asked him what God was inviting him to do, he felt God telling him to replace pride in himself with trust in God. As he confessed his pride and we prayed for God's freedom, a huge smile immediately came across his face. God's grace transformed that simple moment into an experience of profound insight and freedom.

Steve Stewart is a friend who travels the world healing the sick, telling Jesus' story, and caring for the poor. His book begins with this story:

> It was another warm and clear day in southern India, typical for the winter months. I was in a village of about fifteen thousand with a team of forty-five who had gathered from several nations.... We had set up a mobile clinic in a Muslim community that had never had anything like this happen before. In no time, hundreds of people had gathered to receive medical care and, for those who wanted it, the offer of prayer.... . A Muslim lady had brought in her seven-year-old daughter for medical treatment. She told one of our medical team that her daughter had been born completely deaf and therefore had also never spoken. Our team member looked at the women and told her, "I am sorry, but there is no medicine anywhere that will heal your daughter's problem. But I will pray for her and Jesus will heal her." Placing her hands on the girl's ears, she commanded, in the name of Jesus, the deafness to leave. The girl's eyes became wide and she started to look around. The team member, realizing what was happening, spontaneously exclaimed, "Oh God, you are so good!" Immediately the little girl repeated in perfect English, "Oh God, you are so good." Her mother started speaking to her daughter in their native language, Telagu, and with no hesitation or difficulty, her daughter began to speak back to her.
>
> How could this happen? How could a girl who had never heard a sound instantly speak and make herself understood? Only Jesus could do this.[107]

Many of us in our church have travelled with Steve in his ministry, *Impact Nations*, witnessing hundreds of such healings. These demonstrations of God's grace happen at a rate that would surprise those who only get their news from secular sources. Just today I read about people being raised from the dead in India and Pakistan, and

---

[107] Steve Stewart, *When Everything Changes* (Abbotsford: Fresh Wind Press, 2012), 1.

people healed of epilepsy, tuberculosis, and terminal cancer.[108] Whether it is dramatic miracles like these, helping my son, guiding a business decision, or delivering us from fear, God's grace fills our lives with his supernatural, life-altering presence.

For years, although I was a Christian, I did not believe in the transforming presence of God's grace in my life. That changed when I met Robb Powell, a theology student I met in my old dorm. Over the years we would go out for coffee, and I would argue with him over whether God performed miracles in the present-day world. With great skill I explained to him how wanting miracles was a crutch for the lazy and disobedient.

Then one time, after I had won yet another argument, we were sitting in my car and Robb asked if he could pray for me. I remember being bored with his offer but I accepted it to be polite. What happened next changed my life. When he laid his hand on my shoulder to pray for me, I felt spiritual power go through my body. I was stunned, but the only thing that crossed my mind was, "Sick, I lost the argument!" In keeping with my pride, I didn't even let him know what happened to me, but politely said good-bye and drove off to another meeting.

After I drove away, however, the first thing that entered my mind was that I should speak in tongues (this is a prayer language that, five minutes before, I didn't believe in). So all the way to my next meeting, I spoke in tongues, praising God with words I could not understand. After the meeting, I continued praising and worshipping God and became so intoxicated in the Spirit that I could barely drive my stick-shift car home. While I sat in the driveway, unable to move, I remember my landlord knocking on the window and asking, "Are you okay in there?" I replied with slurred

---

[108] *Mission Gateway Magazine* (Fort Erie: Intercede International), Spring/Summer 2012.

speech, "I am oookay." With wobbly legs, I eventually walked out of my car and into a beautifully new experience of God. While such a dramatic experience is not necessary in receiving the gifts of God's grace, this is what happened to me.

The story continues because, since that time, I have experienced countless miracles, especially in seeing people come to Christ. God's Spirit fills me with the power to love others in ways that willpower alone cannot produce. This, coupled with God's reshaping of my character, is continually "saving" me from irrelevance and impotence. This is what God promises to all those who seek his leadership and salvation.

Walking with God

My friend and colleague, Bruce Fidler, says it well, that the central symbol of Christianity is not a cross, but an empty tomb. Christ's resurrection is the distinguishing mark of Christianity. It makes his death meaningful and his promises sure (2 Corinthians 1:20).[109] His resurrection enables us to have a life story that does not end in death, but in an intimate, eternal relationship with God.

How does this relationship change us? Is he just an encouraging friend or a helping hand? It goes far deeper than that: God changes our *identity*. When we are secure in our Father's love, and trust in His divine power, we don't just *act* differently; we are new creations— born again (2 Corinthians 5:17; John 3:3)

This means that I am no longer an orphan looking for a home; I am son who lives inside the love and authority of my Father.

---

[109] "What creation needs is neither abandonment nor evolution but rather redemption and renewal; and this is both promised and guaranteed by the resurrection of Jesus from the dead." N.T. Wright, *Surprised by Hope* (HarperCollins e-books, 2008), Loc. 1803.

> The Spirit you received does not make you slaves, so that you live in fear again; rather, the Spirit you received brought about your adoption to sonship. And by him we cry, "Abba, Father." The Spirit himself testifies with our spirit that we are God's children. (Romans 8:15-16)

Grace is God's provision for relationship. His forgiveness makes us eternally secure and his Spirit makes us eternally significant.[110] Together they reverse the effects of sin, and bring us into a dynamic and life-giving union with Christ.

> Let us then approach the throne of grace with confidence, so that we may receive mercy and find grace to help us in our time of need. (Hebrews 4:16)

As we walk through life, we are never alone. God is with us, in us, leading, comforting, empowering, filling our lives with the sweetness of his presence. Just when we think we grasp the wonder of God's goodness, we experience him in some new way. This is God's salvation: himself, here, forever (Matthew 1:23).

We must rest on this point: salvation comes from being *in* Christ. His gift of salvation is not like a stranger who pays our bus fare. Salvation is not merely a legal transaction where Jesus paid the debt that the Father required. It is more personal than that: "*everything that is Christ's becomes ours by being united to him.*"[111] All humanity is like a rebellious son who forsook his birthright in order to live

---

[110] Eternal security in Christ does not mean that we cannot lose our salvation. However, the way we lose our salvation is not through substandard performance, but through rejecting the gift of grace. Our free will is retained after salvation—we can choose to reject God—but Christ's death and resurrection guarantee that we are secure in God's love for as long as we want to be (Revelation 3:5).

[111] McKnight, Loc. 1359. "Emphasizing union with Christ foregrounds a relational theory of the atonement." Ibid.

independently of God.[112] Jesus is the faithful Son of God who became what we are, so that we can become what he is: one with the Father.[113] Union with Christ *is* our salvation. Through relationship with Jesus we are drawn into the love that is shared between the Father, Son, and Spirit. This is the heart of God's story.

From this we can see how Jesus is the hero of that story. He is more than just a helping hand: he is the source of reconciliation with God (and others). Whenever we write ourselves into the script as the main character, it throws off our whole life story. So while it requires humility to acknowledge Jesus as the hero, it is here that we find the abundant life he promises (John 10:10).

So, will you let yourself be saved today? Will you follow Jesus as Lord and Savior? Will you let God's mercy and grace—instead of your feelings or effort—define your relationship with him? Will you relate to others with a heart of mercy instead of judgment? Will you trust that God's grace is available to inject life's moments with eternal significance? God is always present by his Spirit. Receive his invitation to be your father. God is here with his arms opened wide (Matthew 7:7-8).

---

[112] We are just like Adam and Israel: continually loved by God, and continually rejecting relationship with him. Jesus stands as the second Adam and the true Israel, through whom we can enjoy the relationship he has with the Father (Romans 5:12-19).
[113] McKnight, Loc. 1311. John 10:30.

Chapter Five Discussion Questions

a) Describe the difference between being helped versus being saved, and how we often prefer the former over the latter.

b) If salvation is to deliver us from selfishness, why must it be both a necessity and a gift?

c) To save us, Jesus must be both God and man. He must also be both Lord and Savior. How does Jesus being Lord save us from our selfish existence?

d) From Titus 3:3-7, what does forgiveness save us out of, and what does it save us into? How does forgiveness change how we interact with God and others? Why is Christ's mercy the only way to experience eternal security?

e) Why is grace the only way to experience eternal significance? According to 2 Corinthians 9:8, how does the Spirit of grace change how we approach the needs around us?

Chapter Six
Our Role

So far, we explored how God's story is a true story about Jesus saving us from sin and alienation through his mercy and grace. What we have yet to answer is, how do *we* fit into the story? Are we passive audience members, watching life unfold in spite of us? Do we play the role of a useless son, whose father impatiently says, "Move over, you're too slow"? Gratefully, God has given us a critical role to play. It is summarized in the Great Commandment:

> "Love the Lord your God with all your heart and with all your soul and with all your mind and with all your strength. The second is this: Love your neighbor as yourself. There is no commandment greater than these." (Mark 12:30-31)

God didn't create us to be loveless and useless; he saved us to do that for which he created us—to know his love, and to love others. While our dark side distracts us with petty interests, his powerful love excites our heart, engages our soul, enlightens our mind, and energizes our work. It alone can cause us to truly say, "I am fulfilled."

So what does this life of love practically look like? What do we practically do? We repent and believe.

> "The time has come," [Jesus] said. "The kingdom of God has come near. Repent and believe the good news!" (Mark 1:15)

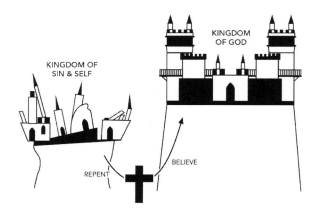

Repentance

The first thing that God asks of us is to repent. What an unfortunate request, for few words carry a more negative meaning! Images come to mind of weeping and wailing, guilt and condemnation. So we must take the time to understand what God means when he calls us to repent. It is then that its meaning is injected with life.

Without a better definition, we will avoid repentance, or seek unhelpful alternatives. We might focus on feeling bad. We might try to make things right. We might blame others for our choices, or harden our hearts. We might cut ourselves or drown our sorrows in the pool of addiction. All of these things are harmful, and none of these things have to do with repentance.

Essentially, repentance is a 180-degree change of heart and mind.[114] If we want to go to New York but are driving 60 miles per hour toward Los Angeles, repentance is not slowing down to 20. We

---

[114] Repentance is "literally a change of mind." W. A. Elwell and P. W. Comfort, *Tyndale Bible Dictionary* (Wheaton: Tyndale, 2001). 1 Kings 8:47 also describes repentance as a change of heart.

must change direction. Repentance is not feeling badly about what direction we are going. It is not trying to be a better driver. It is choosing a new life direction.

What is this new direction? You can imagine by now that it is best described relationally. *Repentance is choosing relationship.* It is a choice to turn from what *breaks* relationship toward what *builds* right relationship. It chooses love over sin. Repentance is less about what we feel or do, and is more about choosing God over self.

One day, an old friend who struggled with alcoholism, came into our house utterly broken. He crumpled on our living room floor, sobbing, pleading for help, lamenting his loneliness. We listened and comforted him for a long while, but I can still remember when his demeanor changed. As we invited him to choose relationship with Jesus over his addiction, he wiped his tears, picked himself up, and slowly walked backwards, telling us that he would be all right, that he was just going through a rough spot. That memory still troubles me. He was sorrowful, he wanted help, but he couldn't believe that exchanging his beer for Jesus was a fair trade.

True repentance focuses less on self and more on how our sinful choices have impacted *God and others* (2 Corinthians 7:11; Luke 19:8). It longs to reverse the effects of our sin. Without love as a motive, repentance is just a religious act that tries to avoid punishment. With love, it is the doorway into restored relationship.

Turning From

We further understand repentance by dividing it into two decisions: to turn *from* and to turn *toward*. First, we turn *from* our sin by confessing and forsaking it (Proverbs 28:13). "Confess" means to admit our wrongdoing, namely that we've broken relationship.

Has anyone ever apologized to you saying, "I'm sorry you feel that way," or "I didn't mean to hurt anyone," or "It wasn't my fault," or "Oops." It is hard to receive these apologies because they lack repentance. Repentance is about *others*. It chooses to value others more than the benefits of sin. It wants to restore the relationship by making things right.

Sadly, repentance is becoming a lost art. We are so conditioned to blame and excuse that we seldom say, "I was wrong." But unless we verbalize our wrongdoing, we cannot experience the freedom of forgiveness or the joy of reconciliation.

Why would we want to repent? *The one thing that sin can never give us is healthy relationships.* Sin might make us richer, happier, or stronger, but it can't reconcile us to God or others. So if we motivate people to repent by telling them how much they are hurting themselves, we make change about *them*. Rather, we must help them want relationship more than the pleasures of sin.

It is a powerful moment to watch someone grasp how their sin has hurt others. Their face changes from either being uncaring or victimized, to deep concern. The natural results of a heart that has repented are often remorse and wanting to make things right (Luke 3:8). The moment of change, however, occurred when they shifted their motivation from self to love.

I find this to be especially true in our relationship with God. We can "repent" with an attitude that says, "Okay, God. I admit I'm wrong... Happy now?" Then, the next time we return to the sin we supposedly repented from, we blame God: "I repented and everything, and you still didn't help me!" One reason we remain stuck in sin is because we're just trying to get out of feeling bad, or we're trying to get back on God's good side, all the while not considering *him*.[115] The only motive that is sufficient for true and lasting repentance is loving God (Psalm 51:4).

---

[115] It is also because they have not believed, but that is the next section's topic.

It follows that if our desire to repent is driven by anything other than love, we're simply swapping one kind of selfishness for another. If we quit our adulterous affair because we don't want to pay alimony, or if we control our anger because we don't want to get fired, we haven't repented; we are still selfish. Deciding to be good instead of bad is equally selfish if love is not the motive. This is why repentance is about *intent* before action—if love is our motive, nearly any action will do.

Not only is an unrepentant heart revealed in being self-serving, it is revealed in our excuses. We never stop a sin that we feel justified doing. If we say, "I know I cheated, but if I don't pass this exam I'll fail the course," we'll cheat again. True repentance doesn't accept any excuse as a good enough reason to sin. The Bible is clear that we all sin, but it is equally clear that we don't *have* to sin:

> No temptation has overtaken you except what is common to mankind. And God is faithful; he will not let you be tempted beyond what you can bear. But when you are tempted, he will also provide a way out so that you can endure it. (1 Corinthians 10:13)

Many factors contribute to our difficulties: people, demonic powers, circumstances, psychological disorders, even ignorance. However, only one factor inhibits God's intervention: sin (Isaiah 59:1-2). Surely, our problems are not entirely our fault, but when we own the parts that are, we give room for God to be our Lord and Savior (Mark 2:17).

The complexity of a problem increases when we dip and dodge, excuse and blame. We hope to avoid guilt, but what we are really avoiding is grace. Simplicity and help increase when we say three words: "I was wrong." This is confession.

Proverbs 28:13 says that after confession, we need to *forsake* our sin. To forsake means to renounce or deny.[116] Clearly, we do not renounce the negative consequences of our sin (we already hate those); what we need to forsake is the benefits and rewards. Therefore, we forsake sin by breaking off our *friendship* with it. I will explain what this means...

As a pastor, people confess their sin to me and I am always humbled by their transparency. In that place, however, I am responsible to help them turn their confessing into forsaking. So sometimes, after people confess their sin, I'll ask, "So, did you like sinning?" Invariably, they look to the ground and say, "Oh no, Pastor Greg, I didn't like it all!" I often respond with a smile on my face: "You're lying! There is only one reason why you sin; it is because you *like* it. So amuse me for a minute and tell me what you like about your sin." With permission to be honest, a twinkle comes into their eye as they describe the pleasures of sin.

Sin is very beneficial. Anger controls. Lust energizes. Gossip comforts. Revenge satisfies. Lies reward. Rebellion liberates. Religion empowers. Independence protects. This is why we sin; it is such a positive experience!

When we verbalize the perceived benefits of sin, we can see two things: how we need Jesus (who can truly meet those needs), and what repentance really is (hating a "friend"). So just as we will not turn from a sin we excuse, we will not turn from a sin we enjoy. But as we grieve the loss of sin's benefits, and want relationship more than those benefits, we find freedom and reconciliation.

---

[116] *The Random House College Dictionary* (Random House: New York, 1984).

Turning To

Once we confess and forsake our sin, we must turn *toward* love and right relationship, first with God and then with others. As non-relational as this might sound, the relationship with God toward which we turn is submitting to Jesus as king, for repentance is first an act of surrender (2 Thessalonians 1:9).

Think of your life as a car. If you invite Jesus into the back seat, he might be part of your life, but he is not leading your life. Even if you ask him to sit right next to you, so you can be closer, you're still in the driver's seat. Repentance is letting Jesus have control of the steering wheel, brake, and gas pedal. Repentance means obeying God's will (Matthew 7:21). It transfers the leadership of our lives from self-rule to Christ-rule.

This is a relational necessity, for how else can self-centeredness be killed? When we submit to Jesus as king, we can then approach him as father and friend, but humility precedes intimacy. For as long as self-rule defines us, we remain his enemy (and love's enemy). Relationship is restored when we humble ourselves and honor him for who he is.

As we've already seen, right order is vital, for *how* I relate to something is as important as *if* I relate to something. If I treat a friend as my lord, or a hobby as my savior; like using a hammer to cut wood, the result will be destructive. Therefore, to rightly relate to God, we must surrender to his love and power.

We can complain, "Jesus doesn't work for me so why should I submit to him?" We must realize, though, that he doesn't "work" if we stuff him in the trunk of our car, bound and gagged! We can't criticize God for having a lack of power in our life when we refuse to give him control. God cannot save what He does not rule. To get on the right side of his love and power, we must surrender our self-rule and submit to Jesus as Lord and Savior. Only then does Jesus "work."

> How does God answer selfishness? It is radical! They execute you at the border and raise you to life on the other side! The gospel executes your self-centeredness! It is fatal! It kills you! Your life no longer revolves around you![117]

Think of your life as a room. As good as you might feel about your life, you protect yourself with walls of rebellion and self-righteousness. You stuff your closet full of guilt and pain that is too hard to face; just when things start going well, the rug of powerlessness gets pulled out from under you. You see the world through a window of mistrust, and your favorite place to sit is in judgment of others. Pride is your guiding light. You tell yourself in the mirror: "I really am a good person," but shame points out every flaw. You work for greed and indulge in lust, but you rest on a pillow of excuses to ease your conscience. This is the dark side of self-rule.

Life of Self

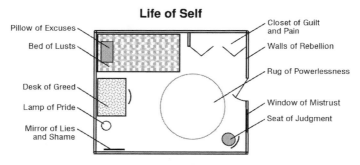

Outside of Jesus, we are trapped in a room we have made through our own selfishness. That room stands condemned, marked for demolition. Jesus does not come to clean that room, change the

---

[117] Winkey Pratney, *The Character of God.* Morning Star School of Campus Ministry, 2003.

décor, or put in new furnishings. He commands us to walk out of that old life, shut the door behind us, and begin a new life that is designed by our creator. And we must leave quickly, for he is committed to destroying every last brick of our sin and pride. Only then will love win, God's leadership be honored, and life be experienced as God intends.

Repentance then, is forsaking all competing lovers and lords (most notably self), and choosing *God's* love and leadership (Luke 9:23). Surrender is good news for he is a safe leader—not just for us, but for all in his kingdom. The result is a place of relational peace and joy (Romans 14:17).

Hence, repentance is more than a one-time decision; it is a way of life. Imagine repentance as a plane flight. Initially, the pilot sets the flight path, but there are constant mid-flight adjustments to arrive at the proper destination. Repentance, then, is a lifestyle of choosing love and relationship over sin and alienation.

In Tolkien's *Lord of the Rings* trilogy, Gollum is a pathetic creature who devoted his life to possessing a magical ring, his "Precious." Who or what is your Precious? If it is not Jesus, it will destroy you as it did Gollum. Our only hope is to hate our "friend" and surrender to the only one who has the right and ability to be our Precious.

Repentance reveals that the first step toward living a life of love is choosing it. This might sound too simple, but there is power in making that decision. When I correct my children, I often ask three questions: What are you doing? What would be more loving? Will you do that now? When they confess their sin and choose love, their hearts are realigned. *Choice* precedes action.

It is easy to focus on *what* we should do, *how* we should do it, if we have the *strength* to do it, or if it is *worth* the effort. All these issues distract us from a very simple choice: will you live in response to

God? It is surprising how a lifestyle of love begins with choosing him in any given moment.

When my wife and I are arguing about something, the argument is typically settled not by a clever compromise, not by "submitting" to someone's power play, nor by demanding that the other person change; it is settled by surrendering our will to God. When that decision is made, a whole new world of options opens up to us.

The heart of repentance came clear to me a few years ago, when we received our foster boys. Before then, my only experience of parenting was raising my natural kids, who had an innate desire to be in right relationship with me. Those four boys, though, did not initially have that bond. Given their painful past, they struggled to choose the vulnerability of connection over the perceived safety of independence. Even though they desired true love, distance, politeness, and rules felt safer.

A foster parent's focus, then, is to build "attachment." As "transplanted" children let their hearts attach to their new parents, love becomes the new currency of that relationship. The result is a relationship that both parent and child find fulfilling.

Ephesians 1:5 describes coming to Christ as adoption. This implies that attachment to our new Father is not innate; it is a choice. That choice is called, *repentance*. Repentance is choosing the vulnerability of trust-filled love, over the safety of a rule-based relationship. This is Zacchaeus' story. When Jesus reached out to him, he was so overjoyed that he repented; he chose to attach.

> Zacchaeus stood up and said to the Lord, "Look, Lord! Here and now I give half of my possessions to the poor, and if I have cheated anybody out of anything, I will pay back four times the amount." Jesus said to him, "Today salvation has come to this house. (Luke 19:8-9)

Zacchaeus' extravagant repentance did not *earn* his salvation. It revealed a heart that attached, that received Jesus' warm invitation into relationship. What if *our* struggle to live a sacrificial life is not because we lack effort or commitment, but because we've not repented, we've not attached? What if we prefer performance and rules because we've not repented/attached? Only as we choose the safety of our Father's love, and rest in our adoption as sons and daughters, will we risk vulnerability and self-sacrifice.

When Christianity feels complicated, God feels distant, or his expectations sound like rules, repent. As we choose to attach our hearts to God and trust in his love, we can step into the next moment together *in* him. That togetherness changes everything, as we will now see by looking at faith.

Faith

The call to repentance reveals the power of choice, so we must not let the complexity of a situation distract us from choosing love. Repentance on its own, however, is incomplete. Wanting something is not the same as having something. We can *want* to be a better Christian, employee, boss, parent, or spouse, but we need more than desire or effort to make that a reality. We need divine help.

It is easy to *not* need God: we just have to lower our expectations, reduce risk, ignore others, and make excuses (Revelation 3:17). Yet self-sufficiency is challenged when our struggles and dreams exceed our ability. Inability is a clue that points beyond itself, for like a pen needs an author, we are designed to need God. The life of love can only be lived by connecting with the source of love.

This is where faith comes in, for actively needing God is something the Bible calls faith. This is why repentance is incomplete on its own; translating choice into action requires faith. *Faith is active trust.*

Sadly, faith is just as easy to misunderstand as repentance. We can treat faith like a formula, where faith is to God what kryptonite is to Superman: it allows us to control him. This is why we get disappointed with God, because our definition of faith differs from his. "Hey, I asked in faith, so why didn't you answer my prayers?" The problem is not God; it is our view of faith.

Shortly after I became a Christian, I began to doubt whether God was real, so I made him a deal. I told him that at 2:30 pm (Pacific Standard Time) the next day I wanted to see an angel. To make it easier for him, I even described an exact location. So I walked outside the next day in eager anticipation of my prayers being answered, but there was no angel. Being an understanding boy, I assumed he was busier than normal, so I gave him another chance the next day. No angel ever came.

This experience taught me a profound lesson. I am not to trust in my faith or in specific results, but in *him* (Daniel 3:17-18). When my confidence is in me or my circumstances, my faith is misplaced, for those objects of faith are not worthy of my trust (Psalm 20:7). But when I trust God, that relationship changes me, even if my world stays the same. So it is for all of us: when we personally trust God to be our source of wisdom, love and power, we are transformed, simply through our relationship with him.

This is why Scripture consistently focuses on the *object* of our faith, not the *quality* or *quantity* of our faith. When Jesus' followers wanted more faith, he focused on God, not on the level of their faith (Luke 17:5-6). Faith in God shifts the focus off ourselves and onto who God is and what he promises his children.

Faith, then, is not how we get God to do what we want; it is how we receive God and his gifts. Faith is not how we *earn* his blessings;

it is how we *receive* his goodness. Imagine trying to hug someone. If their arms are at their side, are they receiving your hug? No, but if they open their arms, are they *earning* your hug now? The answer is still no. They are just *receiving* it. This is what faith is: it is receiving a relationship with God and the blessings that are inherent in that relationship.

The two primary gifts we receive in our relationship with God are mercy and grace. They are invaluable, for they enable us to repent, to turn from selfishness and follow the way of love. Without these gifts, we are unable to repent; but God's forgiveness delivers us *from* sin, and God's Spirit empowers us *to* love him and others (Acts 2:38). In this way God does a very remarkable thing: he *fulfills* our repentance! Therefore, it takes faith to repent, for we must trust that Jesus forgives our crimes and enables us to love and obey (2 Corinthians 1:20).

Repentance and faith are the perfect duo to lead us into relationship. Repentance is a choice to choose relationship over self. Faith is a choice to trust God to fulfill our hope. Together, they create space for God to flood our lives with his grace.

So, as with love, think of faith as a motive (Romans 1:17; 14:23b). It is a way to approach life. Without faith, situations look impossible; we feel inadequate, other people annoy us, and we overspend or overeat. With faith, we pray, try, care, listen, and eat in response to God being actively present in our lives. Faith is why we do *this* instead of *that*.

Picture yourself being invited to climb down a sheer rock face, never having rock-climbed before. Most of us would kindly decline the offer. Now picture yourself with top-of-the-line equipment and a professional instructor and belayer. Trusting in the equipment, proper instruction, and a pro climber might change your mind. This is what faith in God is like. Trusting him causes us to do things that we would not do otherwise.

Often, when I tell stories about the people who have lived in our home and the challenges we face as pastors, or when I tell them that we welcomed six more children into our home, besides our own four, they say that they could never do what we do. I typically think: Don't bother! I'm just trusting that God will empower me to do what he's called me to do, just like he'll grace you to do what he's called you to do. Faith, or trusting in his saving presence, enables us to live a supernatural life.

What does faith in God look like? It looks like basing an action on *him*. I often say to myself, "Given that God *is* love, power, and truth, what is he inviting me to do right now?" Then I make that choice. Some might think that is remarkable (others might think it is silly); for me, trusting in God is the most logical thing to do. When I trust in myself or others I am consistently disappointed. So when I see that my choice is not between trust and not trust, but between trusting God and trusting someone or something less, choosing God always makes the most sense. So if repentance is choosing love, faith is choosing an action based on who God is, in and around me.

From this we can see that faith and action are inseparable— trusting God always looks like something (James 1:22; 2:26). This is why Jesus smeared mud in a blind man's eyes and then told him to go wash it off (John 9:6-7). He gave the man a way to demonstrate the trust necessary to be loved. In so doing, Jesus made that moment about trust and relationship.

Faith shapes our whole life—our health, relationships, finances, future, history, and sexuality—for it looks at life through God's eyes. Some people contrast faith with reason, feelings, or work. Instead, we must let all we think, feel and do be an expression of trust in him.[118]

> Trust in the Lord with all your heart and lean not on your own understanding; in all your ways acknowledge him, and he will make your paths straight. (Proverbs 3:5-6)

Envision a life that is inspired by a healthy kind of expectancy: not about what God should *do*, but about who he *is*.[119] Expect God to be loving and powerful in any given moment. Life is always a mixture of joy and sorrow. However, faith says that even though there are many ways to respond to a situation, doubting God's heart and ability is not one of them. What we find is that when faith is the fence around our thoughts, love thrives (Romans 8:35-39).

Who Do You Trust?

Tim Keller uses the term *functional savior* to describe those things that we practically trust for security and significance. The list of potential saviors is endless: intellect, family, career, luck, fitness, travel, anger, money, or even pets. We like idols or false gods because they act more like consultants than CEOs. They offer help without us having to get out of the driver's seat. The problem is, they only help; they never save. Our minds can't comfort us, mothers die, careers crash, and dogs can't save us (okay, *my* dog can't save us). Instead of trusting karma, evidence, personal effort, or people, God invites us to trust *him*. He alone has the power to deliver us from evil and give us eternal life.

Everyone has faith; the only question is whether the object of our faith is worthy of our trust. Jesus is worthy because he is pure

---

[118] Romans 10:17; James 2:26; 1 Corinthians 5:7; 15:10; Hebrews 11:1.

[119] Paul Barker describes three common substitutes for faith: hope (trusting God for the future and not the present), knowledge (giving mental assent versus active trust), and presumption (moving beyond humility). ENLI, *Life of Faith, Lesson 2,* 2007.

love, unequalled authority, and absolute truth. I have watched the blind see, the adulterer forgiven, the cynic saved, the hurting comforted, the lame walk, the greedy give, the addict freed, and the lazy serve. The miracles of faith and love are countless and varied, but what they all reveal is Jesus, and the beauty of how he saves us.

Conclusion

This is the turning point in God's story, where he calls us to repent and believe: to turn away from sin and self toward his kingdom of love, and to trust in him to save and lead us into that new life. There is no decision more important.

Don't let the seriousness of that decision distract you from how incredible it is. God wants to free us from the bondage of sin and selfishness, restore us to himself, and give us new life. How amazing that God gives us such an incredible opportunity to restore to us all that sin has disfigured or destroyed!

Moreover, our salvation is not only personally beneficial: it injects our life with a new level of meaning. We become ministers of reconciliation, agents of change. Filled with God's grace, we extend God's love and power into others' lives, freely giving what we have freely received. This is living a life of eternal significance.

I am consistently inspired when I hear stories of how love and trust turn even someone's disability into a demonstration of God's glory. I love the wording of 2 Corinthians 12:9, which does not say that God's power lifts us *out* of weakness, but that God's power is revealed *in* our weakness. God is most clearly revealed, not in a perfect life, but in a life that has found Jesus in the midst of brokenness. This is the power of repentance and faith.

So, who do you trust to be your lord and savior? The most important question you can ask is: are they worthy of my trust? The only one who is worthy of our trust is the Lord Jesus. He alone has the ability to be for us what we can't be for ourselves. So will you let God save you from your sin and selfishness? Will you follow his way of love? Will you trust more in his grace than in your performance or circumstances? Doing so requires nothing more than choosing love (repentance) and actively trusting Jesus (faith). The Bible describes the Christian message as good news, for no lips have uttered anything more profound than the declaration that Jesus fulfills our repentance and faith.

Chapter Six Discussion Questions

a)   In the past, what did you think God's expectations of us were? How did you feel about those expectations? What does God ask actually of us (Mark 1:15)?

b)   How has this chapter changed your view of what repentance is? What choice do we make in repentance (1 Thessalonians 1:9)?

c)   How has this chapter changed your view of faith? Why is it true that everyone has faith? What does faith look like (James 2:20-22)?

d)   What does trusting in Jesus look like for you right now? What do you need from him (Acts 4:12)? To trust in Christ, what would you have to *stop* trusting in? Is there anything that is making it difficult for you to value love and relationship with God and others over the pleasures of sin?

e)   What is the result of God transferring your citizenship from the kingdom of self to the kingdom of God (Romans 14:17)?

f)   When should you receive Jesus' saving presence (2 Corinthians 6:2)?

Chapter Seven
The Final Chapter

The Bible is a story. But it is not a fictional story written for our amusement; it is a real story written for our enlightenment. The plot is simple: God is establishing a kingdom of love on earth. The conclusion is certain: he succeeds. (Revelation 21:3)

How does God tell the Bible's story? God tells his story through the lives of ordinary people—sometimes through them and, at other times, in spite of them. This is comforting, for amidst the complexity of human failings and multiple subplots, God succeeds in leading history toward his purpose. The same is true today, for while the Bible is a finished work, his story is not. God continues to write his story as he did in biblical times, through ordinary, flawed people like you and me. In so doing, God includes all of us in his grand story.

It follows that, by knowing the plot and the ending, we can better cooperate with God's storyline. Have you ever wanted to watch a movie over again because, after knowing the end, you could make better sense of the details? This describes the purpose of this chapter. Eschatology is the branch of theology that studies the future. It seeks to explain tomorrow in order to help us live better today.

So what happens after we die? Muslims hope for a paradise that is full of all that is denied them here. Hindus expect to return to earth in a different body, depending on their karma. Atheists believe in complete and immediate annihilation. A Buddhist "hopes after death to disappear like a drop in the ocean, losing one's own identity in the great nameless and formless Beyond."[120] Popular thought wishes for a reunion with loved ones. What do *you* believe? How do you know if you're right?

Turning to the Bible makes sense, for its author knows the future (Psalm 139:16). Yet as helpful as this is, it is full of challenges: fear-mongering, confusion, and speculation, to name just a few (Mark 13:32). Plus, when we read the Bible's imagery of winged beasts and warring angels, it can sound like a science fiction novel. Add to that people's whacky predictions about Christ's return, and society's general unease with death and judgment, and it makes us wonder if such study is worth it.

In spite of these challenges we must press on. As the inventor Charles Kettering is quoted as saying, "My interest is in the future because I am going to spend the rest of my life there." If we practice good Bible study and hold our viewpoints lightly, there is enough that is clear in Scripture to give us a meaningful sketch of the future. So, after studying the primary Biblical views of the future for many years, I would like to share with you what seems to best explain the relevant texts. To start, let's hear a description of how it will all end:

> Heaven in the Bible, is not a future destiny but the other, hidden, dimension of our ordinary life—God's dimension, if you like. God made heaven and earth; at the last he will remake both and join them together forever. And when we come to the picture of the actual end in Revelation 21-22, we find not ransomed souls making their way to a disembodied heaven but rather the new Jerusalem coming down from heaven to earth, uniting the two in a lasting embrace.[121]

---

[120] *Surprised by Hope*, 7.
[121] Ibid., 19.

Ultimately, the hope and plan of God will be fulfilled when heaven and earth, God and his people, finally dwell together forever in unhindered peace and joy. What a beautiful day that will be! So how will this come about? Beginning with the present day, there seem to be three primary ages.[122]

End Times (now) Age of the Spirit	Time of personal decision: who will be your King? The church's purpose is mission (2 Peter 3:9-12).
Kingdom Reign Age of Jesus	Christ returns to rule this earth. Christians will serve and rule in his Kingdom (Revelation 11:15; 20:6).
New Heaven & Earth Age of the Father	Jesus gives the Kingdom to his Father. Final judgment, general resurrection, new creation (Revelation 21:1-4).

Let's work backward through these three ages, beginning with an examination of the end of human history as we know it.

New Heaven and Earth

The transition between this life and our final destination ends with God settling accounts. Justice demands that every sin ever committed be punished and every act of love rewarded:

> The time has come for judging the dead, and for rewarding your servants the prophets and your saints and those who reverence your name, both small and great—and for destroying those who destroy the earth. (Revelation 11:18)[123]

---

[122] Irenaeus (c. 202 AD) helps us in our study, for he was a disciple of Polycarp, who was a disciple of John (Jesus' disciple). Being so close to the teachings of Christ, he provides key insights into what scripture teaches. He describes three great ages, starting with the present. Revelation 19-22 describes a sequence of events in the last two ages: Jesus returns to judge evil (19:11-21) > Satan is bound, Christians are raised to reign with Jesus for 1000 (symbolic) years (20:1-6) > Satan is released and defeated, then the final judgment (20:7-15) > finally, the new heavens and earth (21-22). Irenaeus, *Against Heresies, Book V*, chs. 32-36.

[123] See also: John 5:28-29; 2 Corinthians 5:10-11; 2 Timothy 4:1; Hebrews 9:27; 2 Peter 4:5; Revelation 20:12-13.

How sobering to consider that those who did not receive Jesus' payment for their sins must pay themselves (Revelation 21:8)! How awesome to consider that those who sacrificed for love will be rewarded (Romans 2:7)![124] In both instances, the choices we make in this life determine our final destiny—eternal life with God or eternal death. The story must end with this level of justice or our daily choices are ultimately irrelevant, and God is ultimately unjust.

Although we might like a third option, we must come to terms with the fact that there are only two eternal destinations. Ideas like purgatory, reincarnation, or annihilation are attempts to avoid judgment entirely, or at least delay it (which is appealing if we doubt a positive court appearance). Such is not the case:

> ...people are destined to die once, and after that to face judgment. (Hebrews 9:27)

God removes the option of grey, and calls us to follow Jesus or suffer the consequences. Such clarity is offensive to the rebellious, but for the humble, it is comforting to know that justice will prevail.[125] Let's explore in greater detail these two final options.

Hell

We have described hell as the culmination of our life choices, but what is hell like? Ideas range from denying hell's physical existence, to imagining a way out, to hoping no one goes there in the first place, to two Biblical views: one sees hell as a place of endless, conscious agony; the other sees hell as a place of degrees of punishment that lead to being burned up. The first view believes that

---

[124] Believers will be rewarded for perseverance (James 1:12), earnestly seeking God (Hebrews 11:6), good works (Ephesians 6:8), and faithfulness (Revelation 2:10).

[125] Ravi Zacharias says that God is a cannon, so we must decide what end to be on.

eternal torment is deserved because we've sinned against an eternal God.

The second view believes that eternal life (immortality) is a gift that God gives only to the redeemed, so those outside of Christ will die (cease to exist) once they pay for their sin in hell.[126]

> Dear friends, if we deliberately continue sinning after we have received knowledge of the truth, there is no longer any sacrifice that will cover these sins. There is only the terrible expectation of God's judgment and the raging fire that will consume his enemies. (Hebrews 10:26-27 NLT)

While the effects of sin are eternal (irreversible), the punishment for sin is not, for a lifetime of sin does not deserve never ending torture. Hell, then, is not "an eternal punishing, but a punishing with eternal consequences."[127] Therefore, the punishment that awaits the unrepentant leads to their destruction (2 Peter 3:7).

> He will punish those who do not know God and do not obey the gospel of our Lord Jesus. They will be punished with everlasting

---

[126] In contrast to eternal life, "the NT does not speak of an eternal death... only [of]... the experience of ruin." (Brown, 833). In Jesus' description of hell in Mark 9:48, the worm that does not die refers to maggots who continue to feed on a corpse until there is nothing left—see Isaiah 66:24. Similarly, "unquenchable" fire (Jer.17:27) means fire that is irresistible and cannot be extinguished: it will totally consume what it burns (Mt.3:12). The reference to the eternal smoke of hell in Revelation 14:11 refers to its ongoing testimony against evil, like the smoke of Edom (Is.34:10)—smoke is not still rising in that location. And when Matthew 25:46 speaks of eternal punishment, "eternal" refers to an *age* of retribution versus a *length* of time. "Jesus did not teach, like Plato and others, that the soul was intrinsically immortal and that it would necessarily go on after death." From all this we see that the first death is physical, and the second death is the eventual destruction of the unrepentant.
France, R. T., *Vol. 1: Matthew: An Introduction and Commentary.* Tyndale New Testament Commentaries (Downers Grove: IVP, 1985), 361-362. Brown, *Vol. III* "Punishment" and "Time" (Grand Rapids: Zondervan, 1986), 98-100, 826-833.
[127] David Reagan, Course: *Eschatology*, Northwest Graduate School of the Ministry, 1997.

destruction and shut out from the presence of the Lord... . (2 Thessalonians 1:8-9)

Look how the punishment fits the crime: those who did not choose to know God will be shut out from relationship with him, the final effect of which is complete destruction.

I believe this view presents a form of justice that is more consistent with God's nature.[128] Moreover, it takes the Bible's portrayal of the unrepentant's fate literally—death, destruction, perishing, ruin, rot, and consuming fire mean what they appear to mean: eventual non-existence.[129]

What these two views have in common is that they describe hell as a lake of fire, furnace, bottomless pit, punishment, outer darkness, anger, weeping, torment, and wrath. People struggle over this because it is hard to imagine how "my" sin is "that bad." I appreciate the struggle, but hell upholds the justice we need, for every crime must be paid for; if it is not by Christ's substitutionary sacrifice, then the offender must and will pay (Romans 6:23). The Bible is clear, "It is a dreadful thing to fall into the hands of the living God" (Hebrews 10:31).

In all this, we must trust God to be just in his treatment of sin. While some demand God to explain his actions, this is not as noble as it looks, for it allows them to quietly slide off the stand themselves and assume the roles of judge and jury. Humility requires us to admit

---

[128] "Everlasting torment is intolerable from a moral point of view because it makes God into a bloodthirsty monster who maintains an everlasting Auschwitz for victims whom He does not even allow to die. How is one to worship or imitate such a cruel and merciless God? The idea of everlasting torment (especially if it is linked to soteriological predestination) raises the problem of evil to impossible dimensions." Clark Pinnock, *The Destruction of the Finally Impenitent*, 1992, 15. http://www.onthewing.org/user/Esc_Annihilationism%20-%20Pinnock.pdf (2012)
[129] For a simple and more detailed presentation of this view, see Edward Fudge, 2012: http://www.youtube.com/watch?v=oHUPpmbTOV4

key truths: God is just and we are not, we deserve what justice requires, the absence of eternal consequences erodes virtue, and Christ's sacrifice is our only escape from judgment. When we start with these basics, we can discuss various biblical views as attempts to understand God's justice. As we do, we see hell as not only logical, but as an essential part of God's good and loving leadership.

Let us not be like children who ask what the consequence is for a particular crime. They are not interested in love; they are selfishly weighing if the punishment is "worth it." While the punishment is unimaginable, true repentance not only fears God's wrath; it is ultimately motivated by love. It wants to turn *to* God, not just *from* punishment (Romans 2:4). When our hearts pursue love, we run toward relationship and we see hell for what it is—the just and natural outcome of selfishness and rebellion.

Heaven

Just as hell is better understood through a love paradigm, so is heaven. Some people view heaven as the place to be perfectly selfish—even the streets are gold! Others imagine heaven as a place in the clouds where we chant to a conceited God forever. Apart from their unbiblical sources, such inventions are flawed because they contradict God's nature. The Bible describes heaven as a place of feasting, beauty, riches, and life, all because of one reason: we are *with* God, in a sinless state.

> Then I saw "a new heaven and a new earth," for the first heaven and the first earth had passed away, and there was no longer any sea… And I heard a loud voice from the throne saying, "Look! God's dwelling place is now among the people, and he will dwell with them. They will be his people, and God himself will be with them and be their God. 'He will wipe every tear from their eyes. There will be no more death' or mourning or crying or pain, for the old order of things has passed away." (Revelation 21:1-4)

When we see God for who he is, talk of heaven is less about location, duration, or even activity, and more about a quality of life, namely being with *him*. In *The Great Divorce*, C.S. Lewis describes heaven as a place that is more real than here, for our experience of God will be far wider and longer and higher and deeper than this present world can contain, thus making heaven a timeless experience. So while we taste of God now, our enjoyment of him there will be without restraint. Having this kind of relationship with God is what heaven is truly about. It is divine precisely because of the love within its borders.

Elsewhere, Lewis explains how our lack of imagination makes us content with so much less than what relationship with Jesus gives:

> It would seem that our Lord finds our desires not too strong, but too weak. We are half-hearted creatures, fooling about with drink and sex and ambition when infinite joy is offered us. [We are] like an ignorant child who wants to go on making mud pies in the slum because he cannot imagine what is meant by the offer of a holiday at the sea. We are far too easily pleased.[130]

When our foster boys first came to us, we took them camping at Debbie's family cabin. As we drove over the bridge heading out of town, Yemill, who was five at the time, stared out the window wide-eyed. When we asked him what was so interesting, he simply pointed with his eyes and said, "Mountains." He had never been out of the city before. So, too, with us there exists a reality that is just as unknown and just as magnificent. That reality is relationship with the living God.[131]

---

[130] C.S. Lewis, *The Weight of Glory and Other Addresses* (New York: HarperCollins, 1949), 26.

[131] "If we are even to glimpse this new world, let alone enter it, we will need a different kind of knowing, a knowing that involves us in new ways, an epistemology that draws out from us not just the cool appraisal of detached quasi-scientific

Heaven and hell are the two options our life choices lead us toward. We must decide: will we walk toward relationship with Jesus or not (Proverbs 4:18-19)? Moreover, will we treat these two life paths as seriously as God does? Jesus died that we might be spared the agony and destruction of life *outside* him, and given eternal life *in* him. Let us not be content with selfish fun, self-defined virtue, or avoiding pain. We must shake off our zombie-like trance, and wake up to the immediate and eternal consequences of where our choices lead.

> God will repay each person according to what they have done. To those who by persistence in doing good seek glory, honor and immortality, he will give eternal life. But for those who are self-seeking and who reject the truth and follow evil, there will be wrath and anger. (Romans 2:6-8)

I turned to Christ when I was eleven years old, and I remember being fascinated with the Bible's description of heaven. I was mesmerized by heaven's purity, beauty, and peace. I dreamed of what it would be like to live without sin, with God, in perfect harmony. Forty years later, little has changed. The parable of a man who sold all he had to lay hold of the kingdom of heaven makes sense to me (Matthew 13:44-66). When the way of love seems too hard and the weight of temptation too heavy, I have a hope that lightens my step and lifts my soul. I admit that I need the promise of heaven to endure the trials of life (2 Timothy 4:7-8).

The Kingdom Reign

Between now and our ultimate end, Jesus is establishing his heavenly kingdom on earth. Choosing to participate in his kingdom

---

research but also that whole-person engagement and involvement for which the best shorthand is 'love.'" *Surprised by Hope*, 73.

now is the road that leads to living with him there for eternity.[132] Given its significance, we must ask: what is a kingdom and why is it important?

Romans 14:17 describes God's kingdom as a place of righteousness, peace, and joy. What makes it so is that it is not a democracy, it is a kingdom,. It is precisely because Jesus sovereignly rules his kingdom that it is a glorious place. No competing powers or impurities are allowed to enter (Revelation 21:27).

Years ago, I went to hear Jackie Pullinger describe her work among the poorest in Hong Kong, and she invited a philosopher to speak on political theory. Building off Plato's work, he showed four political systems and their perversions.

Political Systems (listed from best to worst)	Risk	Freedom
a. *Theocracy* – An experience of God (theos) in each person	Absolute	Absolute
b. *Kingship* – Ruled by one good man (king)	High	High
c. *Aristocracy* – Ruled by a class of best (aristos) men	Moderate	Moderate
d. *Timocracy* – Ruled by property owners (timema)	Low	Low
d. *Democracy* – Ruled by voted in representatives of the people (demos)	Low	Low
c. *Oligarchy* – Ruled by a group of a few bad (oligos) men	Moderate	Lower
b. *Tyranny* – Ruled by one bad man (tyrant)	High	Very Low
a. *Ecclesiocracy* – Religious group (ekklesia) uses God to control people	Absolute	None

He explained how the levels of risk and freedom in each system relate to each other. Democracy has low risk because it distributes power to all people, making it the preferred form of civil government

---

[132] *Kingdom* and *church* are not synonymous. The church is a temporal community for Jesus' followers, but the kingdom is the eternal reality. The church serves the kingdom.

today.[133] What might be surprising, though, is that it also has a low level of freedom. This is because when a ruler does not personally protect the people and the people do not trust the ruler, each person must protect themselves through legislation and laws; with each law passed, a little more freedom is lost.

I experienced this when we built our house a few years ago. The architect looked at our original plans and listed all the things we couldn't do—even the height of our basement had to be 7 feet 11 inches, not 8 feet! Of course, bylaws are designed to protect our neighbors, but each law chipped away at our personal freedom.

We must understand that when we don't trust others to keep us safe (especially those with power), we turn to laws instead. With each threat we experience or even anticipate, we add another law. This is why democratic societies have more laws than any other political system—without trust-filled relationships, we seek other forms of protection.

A democratic mindset shifts our accountability from *relationship* to *rules*, where we depersonalize moral responsibility. The problem with rules is that they are not a substitute for trust and love. If we use heartless laws to protect ourselves, we won't experience being personally loved and defended. No wonder sociologists describe our society as having a low-level hum of anxiety in it—our methods of self-protection leave us feeling vulnerable and uncertain.

We see this in families: as trust decreases, rules increase. I explain to my kids that if I can't trust them, then I have to impose more rules on them, to protect the other family members from their selfishness and irresponsibility. But if they choose love, the burden of rules lifts

---

[133] Regarding democracy, Stephen Mansfield quotes John Adams: "Democracy never lasts long. It soon wastes, exhausts, and murders itself. There never was a democracy yet that did not commit suicide." *Egypt: A Contrarian View*, February 14, 2011 (http:// mansfieldgroup.com/category/blog/)

to reveal a life of peace and joy. I learned this growing up. I had more freedom than my foster sister, who lied, stole, and ran away. Rules are necessary when trust and love are lacking.

Can you see where this is going? I am grateful to live in a democratic society, but we must see that there is something better than democracy: a kingdom ruled by Jesus Christ. God's kingdom is revolutionary because it is trust-based, not law-based; it is founded on love and relationship. Because Jesus is pure love, we can trust him to be our advocate, and this trust shapes how we relate to each other. We no longer relate through rules and mistrust, but through love and respect, because we have a common Lord to whom we all submit.

I experienced this personally when the adoption of our son Toby was contested by his birth father. We knew the father wasn't able to care for him but what could we do? Our lawyer outlined the legal options (all of which involved not talking to the birth father), but we arranged to have a personal meeting with him instead. We had a wonderful talk, and in the end, he gave us his blessing to raise his son. Trust and humility enabled us to find the best solution for everyone.

A number of years ago, I watched video footage from Jordan as they mourned the death of King Hussein. I thought it strange that in modern times people would lament the death of a king. Shouldn't they rejoice at the end of a dictatorship and seize the opportunity to establish a democracy? I'm sure reality isn't as idyllic as I'm describing it, but I caught a glimpse of a people who loved their king because their king loved them. The point is that trust and trustworthiness redefine our relationship with power.

When we trust God instead of rules, we exchange limiting, cold, inadequate laws for a warm, secure, freeing relationship. We see this in children. When a child wants to jump from a high ledge, we can create a rule (two feet or lower), or we can smile and open our arms.

This is a taste of heaven—life widens and deepens when we trust our heavenly Father to look out for us. When we shift from a democratic mindset to a kingdom mindset, we find refuge in God's loving leadership.

This explains the significance of Christ's return to earth. At that time, our experience of God's kingdom will grow from an individual to a "political" reality. There will be a personal, loving, powerful king to rule the whole world.[134]

> The kingdom of the world has become the kingdom of our Lord and of His Christ, and He will reign forever and ever. (Revelation 11:15)

The world after Christ's return will differ dramatically from today. Wars will cease and evil will be severely judged (Isaiah 2:1-4; Zechariah 14). There will be rich agricultural bounty, great feasting, pervasive peace, extreme length of life, and harmony between people and animals (Isaiah 11:6-10; 25:6-9; 65:17-25). God's love and power will not just transform *us*, but our social and physical world as well.

I used to think this description referred to the new creation after the final judgment, but I couldn't understand why sin and death were still present (Isaiah 65:20; 1 Corinthians 15:24). The answer is that these passages describe a time *between* this and the final age. No one knows when, but a day is coming when Jesus will return to rule *this* world in the fullness of his authority (Mark 13:32). Let us long for that day!

Christ's earthly reign does more than explain Bible texts; it reveals the importance of today. When he returns, the earth and

---

[134] "There will be no end to the increase of His government or of peace." Isaiah 9:7 Jesus' return will be personal (1 Thessalonians 4:16), physical (Acts 1:11), visible (Revelation 1:7), and powerful (Matthew 25:31). He will rescue believers from wrath (1 Thessalonians 1:10), destroy all sin (2 Corinthians 15:24, 54-57), and establish his reign on earth (Matthew 25:31).

human cultures are redeemed, not destroyed (Romans 8:18-25). Even though saving souls is the priority in this age, it must not be contrasted with personal, relational, environmental, or social development, for they are also potentially eternal. How encouraging it is to know that our lifetime of work on earth is not in vain; for not only will Jesus build upon it, all those who serve him now will rule with him then.[135]

> Blessed and holy is the one who has a part in the first resurrection; over these the second death has no power, but they will be priests of God and of Christ and will reign with Him for a thousand years. (Revelation 20:6)

We must keep on our relational glasses when we read a passage like this. God is not rewarding his favorites with positions of power; he is granting those who have shown themselves as trustworthy servants to continue on. He will honor the faith and love we express now by entrusting us with greater responsibility. Is there a better way for Jesus to find his future leaders than by watching how we love others in his absence (Luke 19:13)?

So do not consider your career as a necessary evil. Do not view earth-keeping or loving the unlovely as wasted endeavors. Not only is there practical benefit in this age, we are being fashioned into trustworthy leaders for the coming age (Luke 16:11).

Nor should we underestimate God's willingness to create the future *with* us, not in spite of us. Pessimistic visions paint a picture of a defeated, disobedient church, but we must have more confidence in God's Spirit than that. Just as Jesus will hand over a

---

[135] Daniel 7:9-28; Matthew 19:28-29; Luke 19:11-27; 1 Corinthians 3:12-15; 1 Corinthians 6:2-3; Revelation 2:26-29; 3:21; 4:1-5:14. This is the first resurrection where the righteous will rise with Christ. During this age, the unsaved will be held in dungeons until judgment (2 Peter 2:4, 9).

kingdom to his Father at the end of that age, so the Spirit will hand over a church to the Son at the end of this age.

Many elaborate theories try to forecast *when* Jesus will return, but God wants us to focus on *why*.[136] Jesus will not return because the world and the church are beyond repair, for that would imply that the Holy Spirit failed. On the contrary, the Spirit will succeed in preparing the world and us for Christ's return (Matthew 24:14).

This vision of the future injects eternal significance into today because our present activity prepares the way for Christ's return. Jesus won't start over when he returns; he will build his kingdom on the faith and love we express today.[137] As we reconcile to God people, ideas, music, institutions, and so on, we prepare this world to meet its king.

In *God's Not Dead*, Rice Broocks gives historical evidence of Christianity's effect on society. He calls it "the grace effect."[138] Even though Christians often misrepresent God, his grace has enabled many to display Christ-like self-sacrifice, generosity,[139] and advocacy. The resulting hospitals, schools, businesses, charities, cultures, legislation, and families reveal the presence and values of God's kingdom. Broocks includes this example:

---

[136] Mark 13:32-33, 35; Matthew 24:36; 1 Thessalonians 5:1-5, 11.

[137] "Redemption doesn't mean scrapping what's there and starting again from a clean slate but rather liberating what has come to be enslaved." "The old field of space, time, matter and the senses [namely, God's creation] is to be weeded, dug, and sown for a new crop. We may be tired of that old field: God is not." "Salvation, then, is not 'going to heaven' but 'being raised to life in God's new heaven and new earth'" *Surprised by Hope*, 95, 162, 197.

[138] "Through the inward transformation of the individual, there is a corresponding outward transformation of society. This is what I call the "grace effect." Rice Broocks quoting Larry Alex Taunton. *God Is Not Dead*, 190.

[139] "The average evangelical [Christian] gives almost *ten times* as much money to nonprofits as the average atheist." Ibid., 201.

> In 1844, J. L. Hastings visited the Fiji Islands. He found there that life was very cheap and that it was held in low esteem. You could buy a human being for $7.00 or one musket. That was cheaper than a cow. After having him you could work him, whip him, starve him, and eat him, according to your preference—and many did the latter. [Hastings] returned a number of years later and found that the value of human life had risen tremendously... . Why? Because across the Fiji Islands there were 1,200 Christian chapels where the gospel of Christ had been proclaimed.[140]

Examples such as these reveal how God's kingdom is already transforming people and societies, but they also foreshadow the day when Christ will fully establish his kingdom on this earth.

> Then the end will come, when he hands over the kingdom to God the Father after he has destroyed all dominion, authority and power. For he must reign until he has put all his enemies under his feet. (1 Corinthians 15:24-25)

On that day, the most amazing thing will happen: God will come to live with us on earth (Revelation 21:1-5). Creation will go through a metamorphosis as sin and death are purged from its nature, and we too will receive new bodies to live with God here, forever (1 Corinthians 15:42-49). This is the fulfillment of God's story: heaven and earth uniting, two worlds becoming one where we live with God in perfect harmony. What a perfect conclusion, for "love is not [only] our duty; it is our *destiny*."[141]

How do we participate in that heavenly kingdom? Through the resurrection of the dead. This is the key to the Christian hope.

> If Christ has not been raised, our preaching is useless and so is your faith... . But Christ has indeed been raised from the dead, the first fruits of those who have fallen asleep.... I declare to you, brothers and sisters, that flesh and blood cannot inherit the

---

[140] Ibid., 196. Quoted from D. James Kennedy and Jerry Newcombe, *What If Jesus Had Never Been Born?* (Nashville: Nelson Publishers, 1994), 27.

[141] *Surprised by Hope*, 288.

kingdom of God, nor does the perishable inherit the imperishable. Listen, I tell you a mystery:... the dead [in Christ] will be raised imperishable, and we will be changed.
(1 Corinthians 15:14, 20, 50-52)

Our hope is not eternal nothingness, nor an endless reincarnation inside what already is, nor an otherworldly escape from the material world; our hope is receiving a new body that is fit for life with God.[142]

The End Times

Working backwards from this conclusion, we can see how this future changes how we live today (2 Peter 3:11-15). Typically, people try to build their own versions of heaven now. It is why we try to buy a nice home or car, raise good kids, give to charities, and drink responsibly (or not). These are attempts to create our little heavens on earth.

In spite of our sincere efforts, why doesn't it work out? Not only are we unable to meet our ideals, our version of heaven eventually conflicts with someone else's: our spouse has different priorities, our kids rebel, the poor cheat us, an addict won't change, or an extremist won't compromise. Their only crime is trying to build their own

---

[142] Colossians 1:13-14; Revelation 11:15-18. The earth will continue, but in a new state. So when 2 Peter 3:5-7 describes the earth being destroyed by fire, it is likened to the flood, which destroyed sin, but not the planet (see also 1 Corinthians 3:12-13).

Do not think of heaven as our eternal home, but as a resting place between our physical death and awaiting our return to earth with Christ. "Paradise is, rather, the blissful garden where God's people rest prior to the resurrection. When Jesus declares that there are many dwelling places in his Father's house, the word for dwelling place is *monē*, which denotes a temporary lodging." Ibid., 40.

Bruce Fidler says that *eternal home* in 2 Corinthians 5:1 refers to our resurrected body. The word *eternal* refers to the quality of our new body, not to a length of time in a specific location (heaven). Again, this implies heaven is not our final home; earth is.

versions of heaven. The reason our heavens collide is because we're all self-centered.

Before I was married, my vision of a "heavenly" marriage was my future soul mate and I, each reading theological books on a porch overlooking a scenic view, then discussing our insights with each other while sipping exotic drinks. Well, my wife doesn't enjoy those books any more than I enjoy playing a role in whatever her fantasy was. What I didn't know is that the greatest enemy of relationship is our personal versions of heaven (what counselors call "conflicting expectations").

By definition, heaven can't be our invention; it must be built by one who can create a truly heavenly kingdom for *all* people. Our hope is for Jesus to bring *his* version of heaven to earth. This implies that the only way that we can taste heaven is if we participate in *God's* kingdom, for this is how self-centeredness is destroyed and love wins.

This captures the purpose of this present age. It is the time to desert our self-centered worlds and build God's kingdom. Our prayer is, "Your kingdom come, your will be done on earth as it is in heaven" (Matthew 6:10). This is both our purpose and our hope. Our prayer is not that God will destroy the earth, but that he will redeem the earth and all who long for his return. Gratefully, we know that this prayer will be answered, for Jesus will succeed in establishing *his* rule on *this* earth.

This future reality describes our present mandate: to prepare people to receive their King. Human history is framed in this context.

> Jesus has apparently been commissioned by the Father to resolve the leadership crisis that currently exists in the universe... . He came to earth with the intent of ending the insurrection of

mankind against the leadership of God! He came to conquer all opposition.[143]

We know this present age is not heaven, for if that were the case, sin wouldn't exist. That time will come, but sin must remain, for this age is designed to serve another purpose: to lead people to repent and believe (2 Peter 3:9). Given that people have only one lifetime, our task is urgent. We must work to bring people into right relationship with God before this age ends and Christ returns in his glory.[144]

Although we wait for that day, we wait eagerly for we know that God's plan will succeed. His rule is steadily advancing and will culminate in the final establishment of his Kingdom on earth, where a people will live in peace under his rule (2 Peter 3:13). Between now and then, our mission is clear and victory assured (Revelation 7:9).

The most rewarding aspect of my life is helping people taste and embrace God's kingdom. There is nothing more exhilarating than watching people abandon their shanty kingdoms and submit to Jesus' love and leadership. I sincerely enjoy my vacations and hobbies, but seeing lives changed makes the pleasures of this world feel like mere shadows of reality. We were built to bring heaven into people's souls.

The Bible's description of the future might sound like a science fiction novel, but unless we understand what lies ahead, life is emptied of ultimate meaning. I asked my children what those games

---

[143] Jan Hettinga, 54.

[144] "The mystery of the Kingdom is this: The Kingdom of God is here but not with irresistible power... the Kingdom of God has come among men and yet men can reject it." George Eldon Ladd, *The Gospel of the Kingdom* (Grand Rapids: Eerdmans, 1959), 43, 39.

are called that have no winners or losers, and their unanimous response was "*boring*." This is why I am not an atheist; I couldn't live with such futility. For good reason the Bible describes life as a race, for we need a finish line to inject life with meaning. Crossing that line will be the most terrifying or exhilarating experience we can imagine, depending on whose kingdom we spent our life building (Hebrews 12:1). In this way, life is emptied of its purpose when heaven and hell are ignored.

The *Newsboys* wrote a song about Christ's return, and I am sobered by one line in particular. Speaking to Jesus, the singer sarcastically remarks,

> When you come back again, could you bring me something from the fridge? I heard a rumor that the end is near, but I just got comfortable here.[145]

I have often wondered how the devoted Jews of Jesus' day—after centuries of study and anticipation—missed the coming of Christ. Then I thought how we have the same potential to miss Christ's second coming, but for the opposite reason: while they expected a king but Jesus came as a servant; perhaps we will expect a servant but Jesus will return as a king. His desire to establish political rule might be unsettling for us, if we think that it betrays his servant heart or desire for relationship. Unless we see that God's commitment to rule is just as motivated by love as was his sacrifice for sin, not only will we misunderstand love, we will reject Christ.

However, if we embrace where God's love naturally leads him, our life direction will change accordingly. We will be able to endure the cost of mercy because we trust in a future justice. We will invest in people's eternal destiny instead of follow our fears. We will weigh our temporal desires in light of a greater vision. Essentially, our

---

[145] The Newsboys, *Lost the Plot*. Album: *Take Me To Your Leader*, 1996.

version of heaven will be abandoned for following a better king with a better kingdom. This is how knowing and trusting in God's future injects today with clarity and conviction.

Chapter Seven Discussion Questions

a) How have you heard people describe life after death? Why is it important to understand the truth about life's final chapter?

b) Describe eternal life, from Revelation 21:1-4. What makes heaven such an incredible place?

c) Why is the existence of hell necessary if God is a God of love? Describe God's justice and why it so critical in the last chapter of God's story (Revelation 11:18).

d) Why is God's kingdom better than a democracy?

e) Knowing that God will build his coming kingdom on our faith and love, instead of destroying this earth and starting over, how does that affect how we live today (Matthew 25:14-30)?

f) Are you prepared to meet God on Judgment Day? How do we have confidence regarding that day (1 John 2:28; 3:21; 4:15-18; 5:13-15)?

Chapter Eight
Living the Story

At the start of this book, we described the chapters as puzzle pieces that form a comprehensive picture of God's story. Here is a summary of "Relational Theology":

- The source of truth is a person, Jesus Christ, who we know objectively through his Word and personally by his Spirit.
- God is relationship (Triune) and we worship him as Lord and Savior for he is unequalled authority and pure love.
- God created us for relationship, where we become secure and significant people as we receive and give his love.
- Sin (selfishness) alienates us, but the self-giving motive of love brings peace. Love is composed of justice and mercy.
- By faith we receive Jesus' fulfillment of our repentance: mercy reconciles us, and his Spirit of grace empowers us to love.
- God will succeed in establishing his kingdom of love on earth.

These truths sum up a relational theology. What remains is answering the question: how do these truths change us? Without an answer, God's story is an interesting idea, not a life-changing reality. Let's explore the answer by looking at one example—our relationship with the church. I chose this topic because many people's biggest problem with God is his church, or "organized religion"; if God can help us here, he can do anything![146]

The church's problems are innumerable: The Crusades and Inquisitions,[147] pedophile priests, divisiveness,[148] hypocrisy, archaic traditions, irrelevance, homophobia, and church services that are powerful sedatives. Yet, even in the face of the overwhelming evidence of dysfunction and sin, God loves the church. This begs the question: has God visited his church lately? Shockingly, the answer is yes. Church as we know it is what God intended. To support this answer, let's define church and its mandate.

Defining Church

The Bible uses three main analogies to describe the church: the Spirit's temple, the Father's family, and Christ's body.[149] Summarizing this Trinitarian outlook, we are a people who love God, one another, and the world: as a temple we worship God, as a

---

[146] 78 percent of Americans believe in a resurrected Christ, but only 20 percent go to church. In Canada, 73 percent believe that Jesus died and rose again, and 10 percent regularly attend church. www.canada.com/nationalpost/newsstory.html? id=f97e6516-f8fe48f6-8d81-81a5f607e2de.

www.religioustolerance.org/rel_rate.htm. Nov. 06.

[147] The Crusades were church-sanctioned military campaigns against Muslims from the 11th to 13th centuries. Around that time, Inquisitions were tribunals used by church leaders to prosecute, torture and even execute alleged heretics.

[148] Christianity has 34,000 separate denominations. David B. Barrett, et al., *World Christian Encyclopedia: A Comparative Survey of Churches and Religions in the Modern World*, (Oxford University Press, 2001).

[149] Erickson, 1045. Note: each metaphor describes more than one relationship (for example, a temple is also a place for the lost and for the community of faith), but for simplicity, I am focusing on one relationship per metaphor.

Regarding being a *temple*, see John 4:23; Ephesians 5:21, 25-27; 1 Peter 2:5. To see how God adopted us into his *family*, see Matthew 10:42; Ephesians 2:19; 1 Timothy 3:15; 5:1-2. To know how we continue Christ's ministry as his *body*, read Matthew 28:18-20; 1 Corinthians 5:18-20; 12:13, 24-27; Ephesians 1:22; 4:11-12.

family we love each other, and as Christ's body we touch the world. So the church is not a building, meeting, program, or organization; we are a *people* who pursue relationship with God and others (1 Peter 2:9). Put another way, we are a community of reconciliation (2 Corinthians 5:18). God commissions us to restore to right relationship whatever is broken or divided. From this we can conclude that the church's only purpose is relationship building.

This means that when Christians kill Muslims, molest children, perform empty rituals, or act like hypocrites, we are not the church. It doesn't matter if we accept Jesus into our heart, read our Bibles, faithfully go to church, or vote for *x*; if we aren't reconciling others, we aren't the church—we're not even welcomed into God's kingdom (1 Corinthians 6:9-10). Obviously, imperfect people are Christians, but don't think God saves those who are committed to selfishness.[150] Therefore, to be a Christian is to commit oneself to a community whose sole reason for existence is to reconcile people to God, one another, and the world. Let's explore how the church is to help us in each of these relationships.

Relationship with God

The church's first purpose is to help people have a healthy relationship with God. Any purpose that replaces this top priority leads the church toward dysfunction, irrelevance, and abuse. We can see this most obviously in the Crusades, where the church had political agendas, but other agendas are equally problematic. If our main purpose is to fight moral or theological error, we will be

---

[150] Remember, the issue is not if we *deserve* salvation (no one does); the issue is if we *want* salvation. God doesn't save us so we can be selfish; he saves us so we can be loving. So if we don't want to love others, we don't really want salvation. Therefore, loving others doesn't *earn* salvation (God loved us first); it is evidence of *wanting* salvation.

legalistic and divisive. If we focus on church growth, we will compromise. When we exalt serving the poor over loving God, they stay victims. If we *primarily* use the church for business contacts, healing, self-improvement, humanitarian aid, enlightenment, friendship, etc., we misuse the church. Even hyper-charismatics are misguided when they pursue an experience of God over the *person* of God. Only the priority of knowing and following God guards the church from harmful excesses.

What this God-worship brings is a new identity. Rather than being defined by our successes or failures, strengths or weaknesses, family or friends, we are defined by our heavenly Father. The importance of this is highlighted when we understand that damaging levels of anxiety, anger, sadness, confusion, or boredom are rooted in being defined by someone or something other than Christ— anxiety, etc., is just how it feels to worship a false god. Just as someone who looks to an addict for love and safety *should* feel unstable, so it is that our emotional instability is evidence that we are standing on shaky ground. But when our identity is in Christ, when he is our source of love, power, and truth, we feel and act differently.

This is connected to the issue of source again. Our source of security and significance determines our level of emotional health. We know this to be true. I feel much differently when an experienced mountain biker tells me that I am a skilled rider, compared to when my five-year-old says the same thing. Likewise, the affirmation of a father is so much more significant than that of a peer. So if we try to feel good about ourselves through positive self-talk, for example, it is no wonder we remain discouraged. Only our creator and heavenly Father can ultimately and rightly define us.

When we rest in the knowledge of being God's son or daughter, we relate to others from a position of strength and humility. We no longer need people's approval because we are already approved by

God. We don't have to be defined by abuse, betrayal, or failure, because Jesus' love defines us (Acts 4:13). We don't have to live in reaction to others or to our personal impressions or our sinful impulses; we live in response to God. No matter what the issue, Christ is the reference point around which we orient our thoughts and feelings.

Therefore, church must have one focus: the *person* of God. Seeking God is more than seeking God as an idea to study, an experience to enjoy, or a force to use, for these subtly shift our focus away from him. It is dangerous to replace God with one of his attributes or benefits, for what is helpful or relevant about God is himself.[151] So even though we need God for salvation, healing, blessing, and so on, these things serve a higher purpose: to have a relationship with him in his kingdom (Matthew 7:22-23; Luke 17:17-18). As a church, this must be our distinguishing characteristic.

This explains what I believe is our main struggle with church: our relationship with God. We come by this honestly, for not only is our society relationally immature, it specializes in offering alternatives to authentic relationships. Pornography, casual sex, video games, alcohol, food, careers, medication, fitness, amusement parks, volunteerism… these are attractive because they offer a *feeling* without a relationship. We enjoy the illusion of security and significance without leaving the comfort of the kingdom of *self.* Many of these things are not inherently wrong, but they become evil when they replace relationship, particularly with God.

Last night, our whole family sat around a campfire, laughing and telling stories. During this time, one of my sons was intently

---

[151] To "know [God] means intimate knowledge, a living experience, a close relation, and not mere acquaintance or theoretical knowledge about God." R. G. Bratcher & W. D. Reyburn, *A translator's handbook on the book of Psalms* (New York: United Bible Societies, 1991), 347.

messaging on Facebook. The next day, we sat down together and I explained to him that he missed an opportunity to connect with us. He responded well when I said that real relationships ask more of us, but there is no replacement for reality. So, too, God invites us to engage with him in the reality of our complicated lives.

Regrettably, churches can be as misguided as individuals. When we fear that God is not enough, we wrap him in practical teaching, relevant music, and engaging activities. It is popular for struggling churches to say that their message is fine; it's just the wrapping. So we seek to put on more "professional" performances. The truth is that we do not inspire insiders or interest outsiders when we offer wrapping paper instead of Jesus (1 Corinthians 2:1-5). God forgive us. There is no replacement for God's presence and power.

Does this mean that churches shouldn't try to be excellent, warm, or inspiring? Of course not, but remember, what makes something good or bad is not *if* it is used, but *why* it is used. When our methods help people personally connect with God, they are well used (Matthew 21:13). In fact, when we really want people to connect with God, we pursue excellence wholeheartedly. The caution, though, is to not forget the goal.

So how does God help us know him? By placing us in his family. As a father, God is with his children, so as I join and participate in family life, I find him (Hebrews 3:6). This can be hard to believe because our society struggles with imagining how more siblings can enhance our relationship with a parent. When I tell people we have ten children, the look on their faces says, "Irresponsible!" (until I tell them that a struggling mom asked us to care for her five children, and eventually, their cousin also joined our family). I'm sympathetic to their response because it wasn't until our family doubled that I realized that having more kids does not lessen their relationship with Debbie and me; it widens it.

When I was younger, my parents invited all sorts of people into our home, sometimes for dinner, sometimes to live with us. This might sound wonderful to you, but I hated it. I would ask, "Why can't we just be a family?" It wasn't until much later that I saw how a full house enhanced my relationship with my parents. When I saw their wisdom, compassion, and self-sacrifice, my experience of them broadened. Moreover, I learned not to be possessive, but to be so grateful for my parents that I wanted to share them with others. Like watching a sporting event with friends, I enjoyed my parents more when it was a shared experience.

So it is with church. The only time my spiritual family hurts my relationship with God is when I have a small view of relationship. However, when *love* defines my relationship with God, church becomes a wonderful place to know and experience him. *Without* community, I get lost inside my own thoughts, feelings, and experiences, and I try to possess God for myself; *with* community, I have a broader and deeper experience of God.

Relationship with One Another

There is no such thing as a just-me-and-Jesus Christianity. Christ's followers are temple stones, body parts, and family members, for our relationship with God and his family are woven together.[152] This doesn't mean lonely lighthouse keepers can't follow Christ; it means self-centered people can't follow Christ, for following Jesus is a relational experience.[153]

Honestly, leaving self-centeredness and embracing community is not easy, for inherent in any relationship is uncertainty and hurt

---

[152] When Adam was sinless, in perfect harmony with God, God said it wasn't good for him to be alone, implying that God wasn't enough to cure his loneliness (Genesis 2:18).

[153] "Whoever claims to love God yet hates a brother or sister is a liar." (1 John 4:19b)

and conflict. And the natural reaction to pain is to react in one of two directions—fight or flight—neither of which lead toward relational health. Even more troubling is how choosing these reactions makes us part of the problem, causing us to multiply the very hurt we're reacting against. The result is a cycle of hurt that feeds on itself.

We reverse this downward spiral by having a new perspective on conflict. We must see that conflict itself is not inherently alienating; it is our *response* to conflict that creates division (Proverbs 15:1). More than not being inherently bad, God uses conflict to mature us:

> No discipline is enjoyable while it is happening—it's painful! But afterward there will be a peaceful harvest of right living for those who are trained in this way. (Hebrews 12:11)

This explains how God designs Christian community. He purposely places us inside an imperfect community to shape us into truly loving people. This often runs contrary to what we think is best for us. Create an image in your mind of the perfect church. Let's call it *iChurch*. You love the music and the teaching. The programs are tailored to fit your needs, and if you want to serve the poor, they'll make it as painless as possible. The best part is the people: everyone is kind of like... you.

With this picture in your mind, ask yourself: will this kind of church help you mature in love? The answer is no. The only way to learn generosity or forgiveness is to be with people who need generosity and forgiveness—otherwise known as people who are needy and sinful! Welcome to church.

God's most effective way to mature us is Fred. Fred is awkward. He publicly scratches where he shouldn't scratch, and picks what he shouldn't pick. He smells in many ways and likes making noises.

Even though you have nothing in common with him, Fred wants to be your best friend.

Fred is God's gift to you. Why? God uses him to teach you about true love. When we are faced with having to love unlovely people, we learn that true love is not based on the worthiness of the recipient. Genuine love is indiscriminate—it doesn't love one and not another, for conditional love is not love at all. Therefore, God uses the relational tension inside community to purify our love, and to increase our need and appreciation of God's love.

Church is an uncomfortable, messy place, but the struggles we experience there teach us more about mercy and grace than any sermon or book ever can. "Good" churches, then, invite and equip us to engage in real relationships.

So why do *you* struggle with church? Are there one too many Freds? Do you feel like a Fred? Are you bored or lonely? Are you undervalued or misunderstood? Do you see sin and error in the church? If your response to these struggles is to withdraw or attack, you must realize the cost of self-protection:

> There is no safe investment. To love at all is to be vulnerable. Love anything, and your heart will certainly be wrung and possibly be broken. If you want to make sure of keeping it intact, you must give your heart to no one, not even to an animal. Wrap it carefully round with hobbies and little luxuries; avoid all entanglements; lock it up safe in the casket or coffin of your selfishness. But in that casket—safe, dark, motionless, airless—it will change. It will not be broken; it will become unbreakable, impenetrable, irredeemable. The alternative to tragedy, or at least to the risk of tragedy, is damnation. The only place outside Heaven where you can be perfectly safe from all the dangers and perturbations of love is Hell.[154]

---

[154] C.S. Lewis, *The Four Loves* (New York: Harcourt, 1960), Loc. 1438.

At this point, someone might say, "Ah, are you saying that we should stay in abusive relationships or dead churches?" No, I am saying that Jesus models a better way to respond to conflict. How did he respond to *our* sin and betrayal? He left heaven and moved in with us. The risk is tremendous, but is there any other way to conquer evil?

> Do not repay anyone evil for evil. Be careful to do what is right in the eyes of everyone. If it is possible, as far as it depends on you, live at peace with everyone. Do not take revenge, my dear friends, but leave room for God's wrath, for it is written: "It is mine to avenge; I will repay," says the Lord. On the contrary: "If your enemy is hungry, feed him; if he is thirsty, give him something to drink. In doing this, you will heap burning coals on his head." Do not be overcome by evil, but overcome evil with good. (Romans 12:17-21)

We all have good reasons for why we sin. A husband says that he has to hit his wife because she's so unreasonable. A rebellious teenager thinks her parents are idiots. Church members leave because they think they have found an *iChurch* just minutes from home. A friend gossips about a friend who has hurt her. A criminal believes in his innocence, not because he didn't commit the crime, but because he feels justified. There is only one problem with our logic: *we still sinned.*

We thrive in community only if we take responsibility for our choices and choose to trust Christ and follow his way of love. If someone treats us poorly or in a way that is hurtful or harmful, God empowers us to walk in an opposite spirit.

I had been a Christian for just over a year when an older boy at school began to make a habit of bullying me. We were on the same bus going to school, and every day that bus felt like a torture chamber. When my brother came home from university for Christmas break, I tearfully told him my story of verbal and physical harassment. He listened kindly, paused, and then said the opposite of what I wanted to hear: "Greg, the Bible tells us to love our enemies, so I think you should give this guy a Christmas present of something that means a lot to you." What?! I was expecting my big brother to apply some of his muscle to the situation, not to set me up to be a wimp!

Well, I took my brother's advice, and so, on the last day before the holiday break, I got off at the bully's bus stop. With my heart pounding, I mumbled something about Merry Christmas and handed him a gift: a Hardy Boy book (my favorite), and a Christian comic. Then I hurried away.

During the whole Christmas break, I was full of fear. I couldn't imagine what the bully would do, now that I had appeared so weak.

I'll never forget that first day back at school. He saw me from across the way and said, "Hey, Greg!" Uh-oh, here it comes. "Thanks for that present. I read the comic, but I haven't read the book yet."

That's it? No mocking remark? No threats? Not then, and not ever. At least in this instance, good overcame evil.

Typically, our choice to withdraw from relationships feels like a logical decision that just so happens to minimize personal cost and maximize personal benefit. We aren't trying to be selfish; we're just being wise. We aren't defensive; we just hate being judged. We aren't lazy; we just have different priorities. How can hurt or discomfort be God's will? God wouldn't ask us to sacrifice for someone who is ungrateful or irresponsible, would he?

Such reasoning ensures a loveless life. When we experience church from a self-centered orientation, we interpret an invitation to unity as a call for conformity. We perceive constructive criticism as rejection. We feel threatened by differences, and we don't trust leaders. In essence, we take things *personally*. This causes us to react to people's perceived selfishness by being selfish![155] Truly, the self-centered can't stay in church because it is a violating experience. And, yes, it is. God designed church to kill our selfishness.

Fortunately, Jesus saves us from self-centeredness. He doesn't just give us better laws with which to control ourselves; he gives us a new nature, identity, and orientation, enabling our thoughts and actions to revolve around Jesus, not ourselves. Through his eyes, we have a perception of others (and him) that leads to relationship:

> So from now on we regard no one from a worldly point of view. Though we once regarded Christ in this way, we do so no longer. Therefore, if anyone is in Christ, the new creation has come: The old has gone, the new is here! All this is from God, who reconciled us to himself through Christ and gave us the ministry of reconciliation. (2 Corinthians 5:16-18)

What great news! We can now respond to others in ways that lead to reconciliation. We can enjoy diversity without feeling threatened, unity without fearing conformity, feedback without assuming rejection, and vision without feeling condemned. We can even respond to being sinned against with compassion instead of insult (Luke 23:34; Hebrews 12:4-11; 1 Peter 4:12-19). In this way, Jesus frees us to receive and give love. This is the purpose of Christian community: it is a place to experience God's grace.

Today's church, then, is God's perfect design, but what makes it a positive or negative experience is how we respond to it. When we receive it as a gift from our loving Father to mature us into people of love, spiritual family becomes the place we've always longed for. And the result is more than an enjoyable experience for us. We display to the world the power of God, for there is nothing more

---

[155] God gives us over to our perceptions (Psalm 18:25-27; 81:12; Romans 1:28). In this sense we create our own alienation and hell.

miraculous than unity inside an imperfect, diverse community of faith (John 17:23).

Loving the World

When we consider the destiny of the lost, not demonstrating or declaring God's salvation is a death sentence. God will judge us for such irresponsibility:

> "You, son of man, are the watchman.... If I say to the wicked, 'Wicked man, wicked woman, you're on the fast track to death!' and you don't speak up and warn the wicked to change their ways, the wicked will die unwarned in their sins and I'll hold you responsible for their bloodshed. But if you warn the wicked to change their ways and they don't do it, they'll die in their sins well warned and at least you will have saved your own life." (Ezekiel 33:7-9, The Message)

As critical as loving the lost is, embracing that lifestyle is filled with complications. Our lack of time and skill, our fears and failures, not to mention their suspicion or even hostility, tempt us to withdraw into a cocoon of guilt and frustration.

In the face of these obstacles, church leaders try to help. They present detailed strategies, in-depth training, inspiring speeches, costly events, and sentences beginning with the word "Just... ." There is a time for this kind of help, but it often doesn't achieve the desired result. Why? These "solutions" have the potential to distract us from the heart issue.

How do our hearts change to where loving the lost is a privilege and a joy? It starts with being honest. Are you honest about the outcome for the lost? Do you see what *God* did to draw them to himself? Do you let your laziness concern you? There is one reason above all others for why we don't help the lost: we resist the loving presence of God in our lives. Even though all the complications are true, the core issue is not about them at all; it is about our relationship with God.

As we open ourselves to God, and let his truth and love soften our hearts, we see the choice to love the world as a choice about whether we love God and are grateful for his love (Matthew 25:40). This is repentance; and as such, it is a *choice*. Love does not wait for a feeling of compassion (or guilt), or for a certain level of confidence. It is a decision based on something better: God's command. We love because he first loved us (1 John 4:19-21). Repentance simplifies the complexity of love to a single choice. Such simplicity upsets only the disobedient.

To be clear, this decision does not guarantee results; it does not promise to meet other people's expectations of us, nor does it determine exactly what we might do. It simply aligns our heart with God's. Yet this is what matters, for in that place we create space for God to save us from a loveless life.

Repentance naturally leads to faith. When we know that we can't achieve what we long for (to be reconciled to the one our heart loves), we cry out to God. This is a perfect conclusion, for the fruit of repentance is not anxious work; it is trusting God to fill our words and deeds with his supernatural love and power. In Jesus, the burden of expectations lifts, sacrifice is a joy, and the help from our leaders that once felt manipulative is now welcomed. Therefore, our faith is not in our effort, training, excellence, strategies, or zeal; it is trusting that although we are weak, Jesus is strong (1 Corinthians 2:1-5).

While the opposite of repentance is lovelessness, the opposite of faith is fearfulness (Mark 4:40). Fear is faith's enemy. It undermines our ability to love the world. For fear of being harmed or polluted or influenced, we disengage from science, homosexuals, humanitarianism, business, turmoil, entertainment, pubs or politics, forgetting that uncleanliness is about our hearts, not our surroundings (Mark 7:15). For fear of being rejected or used, we peer out at the world through stained glass windows, forgetting that whoever tries to save his life will lose it (Matthew 16:25). For fear of being judged by God, we throw crumbs of kindness to the lost in the hope that we will appease God, not realizing that we have only deceived ourselves (Jeremiah 17:10). For fear of not performing well, we withdraw into defeat (Matthew 25:25). We need to see that fear is nothing more than faithlessness, where "risk management" renders us impotent (Luke 19:21-23).

The good news is that faith conquers fear. Faith remembers what fear forgets. It acknowledges that when we are weak, God is strong (2 Corinthians 12:10). It knows that in spite of sin's stain, God made the world good and he is still present in it (Romans 1:20).[156] Faith focuses on what is excellent or praiseworthy (Philippians 4:8). It knows that God doesn't love the world at arm's length; he enters our mess (John 1:14; 3:16). Faith remembers how the religious condemned Jesus for enjoying dinner with sinners (Matthew 11:19). It insists on believing that God has given us all we need to be ministers of reconciliation (2 Peter 1:3). While fear renders us unattractive, irrelevant, and cursed (Deuteronomy 27:19), faith makes us beautiful, effective, and blessed.

When we receive faith, a surprising thing happens: we love what God loves. The caricature of evil we construct in our minds crumbles when we see faces with names—it is not that we are blind to their sin, but we focus more on God's love for them than on how God's image in them has been disfigured. This turns what we

---

[156] "'The world' is always, and emphatically, *God's* world—the order of things which he made, which he owns, and which he rules, despite all his creatures' efforts to cast off his sway." J. I. Packer, *God's Words* (Downers Grove: InterVarsity Press, 1981), 58.

previously thought of as self-sacrifice into grand opportunities to reveal just how much God loves them. Faith conquers love's costs.

> Because we loved you so much, we were delighted to share with you not only the gospel of God but our lives as well. (1 Thessalonians 2:8)

Earlier today I chatted online with a friend who I haven't seen for a while. When I first met him, he was working as an interior designer. From his sincerity to his humor, I really enjoyed him. My favorite line of his was: "Greg, I don't repeat gossip, so I'm only going to say this once." I remember the day when he told me that he was going to hell because he was gay. All I knew to say was that I was more interested in him than in his sexual orientation, and that I really appreciated our friendship. And so our relationship grew.

Over a year later, when he was jobless, and he and his boyfriend had broken up, he had no place to stay. So after much prayer and discussion, Debbie and I invited him to live with us, and he nervously accepted our offer.

His time with us was delightful. Not only did we thoroughly enjoy his company, our kids loved him. He would play silly games with them, and they ate up every moment of it. I still remember the puppet show they put on for Debbie and me one evening.

Then, just before he left to work on the cruise ships, he sat me down to tell me that he laid down the gay lifestyle. Surprised, I asked him why. He said people usually kept their kids away from him because, in his observation, they assumed that all gays are pedophiles. But because he was able to live with our family, he said he experienced a better love. His words helped us realize that regardless of someone's struggles, God's love is always the answer.

When we practice faith-filled love, we become a pleasant fragrance to the world around us (2 Corinthians 2:15). We trade being people's judge for being their advocate. We exchange being a stumbling block on their journey toward Christ to being a path through the wilderness (Mark 1:3). As we love people at their point of need, we don't compromise our standard of righteousness; the opposite is true: we raise *our* standard of righteousness by loving the needy (Titus 3:14). We offer a way for people to see and embrace God's way of love (Matthew 5:16).[157] This is what the church (you and I) is: not a dry and heavy weight to the lost, but an avenue of hope to a dry and heavy world (John 1:5).

As God's love grows in our hearts, many things change. We become more interested in listening to people's stories than winning arguments, we pray because we want them to have more than what we can give, and we find joy in suffering because love has freed us from our fears. What a privilege it is to discover the unique (and exhilarating) ways in which God calls us to extend his kingdom into the world.

One of these ways for Debbie and I is to take in foreign students to live with us. One of our first students was a young man from Japan. He was mostly into partying and snowboarding and eventually he ran out of money. So we decided to let him live with us for free, and this began to open his heart. I can still picture him listening to my wife worship at the piano and describing in broken English how it made him feel. Eventually, we gave him a Bible and we would talk about Jesus; but whenever we asked him what he thought about responding to Christ, his reply would be, "More study."

That all changed when my wife was praying for him one night and sensed God saying that the young man's new girlfriend was pregnant. Debbie sat down with him the next day and told him, "Your girlfriend is pregnant."

---

[157] I love a song by The Newsboys that describes Christianity as a world-transforming party: *Wherever We Go,* The Ultimate Collection, 2009.

"How you know?!" was his response. When she told him that God knows and cares about every part of his life, he chose to follow Christ just a few days afterward. That miracle changed his heart.

As great as that moment was, his joy was short-lived because his girlfriend's family demanded that she get an abortion or they would disown her. Nevertheless, in spite of the pressure, they decided to keep the baby. To support their decision, we invited her to move in upstairs, while he roomed downstairs. More than this, we prayed with her that God would open her parents' hearts to be reconciled again.

A few weeks later, on Christmas Day, she received the most unexpected present. Her parents phoned to tell her that they had decided to accept her and their future grandson back into the family. The next day she became a Christian, and over the next few months we baptized them, married them, and were there for the birth of Joshua. Eighteen years later, it feels like a cycle is complete as that child is returning to visit us for the first time since his birth, as a follower of Christ.

God's love transforms our relationship with the lost. Perhaps what is most surprising is that when we reach out, *we* find God, for he dwells among the least, the last, and the lost (Matthew 25:45). The magic of trusting God is that he doesn't save just them, he saves us—delivering us all from our pride, selfishness and fears, for we discover that we are as poor and lost as those we reach out to. The result is living a life that is best described as *reconciling*.

> All this is from God, who reconciled us to himself through Christ and gave us the ministry of reconciliation. (2 Corinthians 5:18)

This mission clarifies that *we* are the church. As we act as Christ's heart and hands, extending his love into people's lives, we experience Christian community. This also clarifies why we can feel distant from community: we don't join in its mission. A church family is like a sports team, where being part of the team means being out there on the field.

It is a great tragedy to think that community and mission, security and significance, receiving and giving love, are independent versus reciprocal. They inform one another. In our church, we find that when we include the mission as part of people's conversion experience, their relationship with God and his church is dramatically enhanced. Because God is on a mission; to be with him and his family requires participating in his purposes.

Church is more of an adventure or journey than it is an event. So if we feel disconnected or unappreciated, the solution is not to demand more attention, but to obey Christ's call to love the lost. Rick Warren describes the North American church as having a big head and butt, with little arms and legs. When we humble ourselves and participate in the mission of a local church, however, we become balanced, healthy, and whole people.

Conclusion

Proverbs 27:8 says, "Like a bird that wanders from her nest, so is a man who wanders from his home." To wander means to be aimless, idle, or astray.[158] It is a sign of God's judgment.[159] Many Christians are cursed with lonely, dry and fruitless lives, because they wander from their local church. They come to God on their own terms, protect themselves from transparent relationships, and reject the mission of the church.

---

[158] Merriam-Webster's Collegiate Dictionary (11th Edition).

[159] Jeremiah 14:10; Psalm 107:4-5. Listen to God's curse upon Cain: "When you cultivate the ground, it will no longer yield its strength to you; you will be a vagrant and a wanderer on the earth.... Then Cain went out from the presence of the Lord, and settled in the land of Nod."(Genesis 4:12, 16). The word "nod" literally means "wanderer."

Selfishness is at the root of a wandering heart: "He who separates himself seeks his own desire, he quarrels against all sound wisdom." (Proverbs 18:1) In contrast to wandering tumbleweeds are planted trees:

> The righteous man will flourish like the palm tree, he will grow like a cedar in Lebanon. Planted in the house of the Lord, they will flourish in the courts of our God. They will still yield fruit in old age; they shall be full of sap and very green. (Psalm 92:12-14)

When we are rooted in a local church community, we receive the nourishment and pruning we need to live fruitful, abundant lives (Hebrews 10:24-25). So we must ask ourselves, "Do I want to be a tumbleweed or a tree? Will I give up being a self-defined person, blown about by personal feelings and opinions? Or will I put down roots and receive the life of God through the ministry of his church? Will I adopt the church's mission as my own?" God presents to us a promise and a warning:

> God makes a home for the lonely; He leads out the prisoners into prosperity, only the rebellious dwell in a parched land. (Psalm 68:6)

God will provide a wonderful home and prosperous future for people who will humble themselves and join the worship, community, and mission of a local church. So will you be a temple stone, family member, and body part?[160] Will you give up your autonomy and join a spiritual family? Our personal destiny is realized inside this corporate identity. This is what God offers us today.

---

[160] In Biblical times, rocks in a field were called *dead* stones, and those that were cut and chiseled to fit into a wall were called *living* stones. 1 Peter 2:5 describes us as living stones, fitted together to be a house where we dwell together with God and his family. It is death to remove ourselves from the relationships above, below, and on either side of us.

What's Next?

At the beginning of this book, I described each chapter as a puzzle piece, which together form a picture of love—its source, shape, and impact. The title of that picture is Relational Theology.[161] With that picture complete, how should you respond? Should you think more about these ideas? Should you try to apply them to areas of your life? Maybe you could help someone else with them.

As good as these options are, something needs to happen first. Do you remember the challenge I gave you in the introduction? "You have a rare chance to do more than tweak your life; you have an opportunity to change it." How does that occur? It begins with a choice: *will you choose love as your life motive*? Positively answering that deeper question changes you in ways that "tweaking" thoughts or behaviors can't, for it redirects your life away from self-centeredness, toward a radically bigger and better purpose.

Choosing love (repenting) does many things. First, love will lead you to its source: Jesus Christ. It is impossible to live in right relationship with God and others without Jesus being the foundation upon which you build those relationships. Whether you are a seasoned saint or a sincere seeker, humble yourself and need a relationship with Jesus that he controls instead of you.

Second, that choice will catch you up in God's story. This short book is really an introduction to further chapters that God wants to write through *your* life. As you participate in *his* storyline, your personality, experiences, abilities, relationships, dreams... will weave together in ways that fulfill you *and* bless others. All that lies behind and ahead of you will be redeemed when you follow the right storyline.

---

161 Thank you to Keith Swayne for coining this phrase.

While society often sidelines Christianity, it does so at its own peril, for nothing on the horizon can replace the love and leadership of the Lord Jesus. Your choice to join with others in following God's story will show society where its hope lies. Imagine a generation of love-inspired, Bible-led, Spirit-indwelt believers welcoming God's kingdom into every sphere of life! This dream becomes reality with that first choice. God bless you as you make that decision now.

Chapter Eight Discussion Questions

a) What is your experience of church and "organized religion"? What have those experiences led you to believe? How does the presentation of church in this book challenge or reinforce your beliefs?

b) Why is it worth putting in the effort to engage in a spiritual family? What would a healthy relationship with a church community practically look like for you (Acts 2:42-47; 2 Corinthians 6:11-13)?

c) What ideas in this book have you found to be most challenging and most helpful? What is the difference between tweaking your life and letting God transform your life?

d) What does 1 Corinthians 16:14 invite you to do? Why is that choice necessary before working on specific parts of our lives?

e) What are your next steps in moving toward greater relational health with God, with your natural and church family, and with those who don't know Jesus?

f) What will help you succeed with those steps? How can we pray for you?

To find more resources and materials written by Dr. Greg W. Mitchell, go to 12-2resources.com.

Bibliography

Barrett, David B. et al. *World Christian Encyclopedia: A Comparative Survey of Churches and Religions in the Modern World.* Oxford: Oxford University Press, 2001.

Barth, Karl. *Church Dogmatics Vol.III:2.* Edinburgh: T & T Clark, 1957.

Bonhoeffer, Dietrich. *Christ the Center.* San Francisco: HarperCollins, 1978.

Bonhoeffer, Dietrich. *The Cost of Discipleship.* New York: Collier Books, 1963.

Bratcher, R. G. & W. D. Reyburn. *A translator's handbook on the book of Psalms.* New York: United Bible Societies, 1991.

Bray, Gerald. *God is Love, A Biblical and Systematic Theology.* Wheaton: Crossway Books, 2012.

Bromiley, Geoffrey W., gen. ed. *The International Standard Bible Encyclopedia, Revised.* Grand Rapids: Eerdmans, 1988, 2002.

Bromiley, Geoffrey W., gen. ed. *The International Standard Bible Encyclopedia.* Grand Rapids: Eerdmans, 1986.

Broocks, Rice. *God's Not Dead.* Nashville: Thomas Nelson, 2013.

Brother Yun. *The Heavenly Man.* Manila: OMF Literature, 2003.

Brown, Colin, gen. ed. *Dictionary of New Testament Theology Vol. 2.* Grand Rapids: Zondervan, 1986.

Chester, Tim, and Steve Timmis. *Total Church.* Wheaton: Crossway Books, 2008.

Crabb, Larry. *Effective Biblical Counseling.* Grand Rapids: Zondervan, 1977.

Dunn, J. D. G. Vol. 38, *A: Word Biblical Commentary: Romans 1-8.* Dallas: Word, 2002.

Ellul, Jacques. *The Technological Society.* New York: Vintage Books, 1964.

Elwell, W. A., and P. W. Comfort. *Tyndale Bible Dictionary.* Wheaton: Tyndale, 2001.

Erickson, Millard J. *Contemporary Options in Eschatology.* Grand
    Rapids: Baker House Books, 1987.

Erickson, Millard J. *Christian Theology.* Grand Rapids: Baker, 1998.

Fausset's Bible Dictionary. "Biblesoft," 1998.

Fee, Gordon. *Empowering Presence.* Peabody: Hendrickson
    Publishers, 1994.

France, R. T. *Vol. 1: Matthew: An Introduction and Commentary.*
    Tyndale New Testament Commentaries. Downers Grove:
    InterVarsity Press, 1985.

Frankl, Viktor E. *Man's Search for Meaning.* Boston: Beacon Press, 1959.

Gay, Craig M. *Cash Values.* Grand Rapids: Eerdmans Publishing: 2003.

Gee, Donald. *Spiritual Gifts in the Work of the Ministry Today.*
    Springfield: Gospel Publishing House, 1963.

Grenz, Stanley J. *Created for Community.* Wheaton: BridgePoint, 1996.

Grenz, Stanley J. *Rediscovering the Triune God.* Minneapolis: Fortress
    Press, 2004.

Grenz, Stanley J. *The Social God and the Relational Self.* Louisville:
    Westminster Knox Press, 2001.

Griffiths, Michael. *Serving Grace.* Berkshire: Cox and Wyman, 1986.

Grudem, Wayne. *Systematic Theology.* Grand Rapids; Zondervan, 1994.

Gunton, Colin E. *The Promise of Trinitarian Theology.* Edinburgh: T &
    T Clark, 1991.

Hadland, Beverly J. *Hang onto your Hormones.* Toronto: Life Cycle
    Books, 1992.

Hettinga, Jan. *Follow Me.* Colorado Springs: NavPress, 1996.

Hjalmarson, Leonard. *No Home Like Place,* 2013. Draft Ed.

Irenaeus, *Against Heresies, Book V.*

Keller, Timothy. *King's Cross.* New York: Penguin, 2011.

Keller, Timothy. *The Reason for God.* New York: Dutton, 2008.

Kennedy, D. James, and Jerry Newcombe. *What If Jesus Had Never
    Been Born?* Nashville: Nelson Publishers, 1994.

Koenig, John. *Charismata: God's Gifts for God's People.* Philadelphia:
    Westminster Press, 1978.

Ladd, George Eldon. *The Gospel of the Kingdom.* Grand Rapids:
    Eerdmans, 1959.

Lewis, C.S. *Mere Christianity.* HarperCollins e-books.

Lewis, C.S. *The Four Loves.* New York: Harcourt, 1960.

Lewis, C.S. *The Quotable Lewis.* Carol Stream: Tyndale, 1989.

Lewis, C.S. *The Weight of Glory and Other Addresses.* New York: HarperCollins, 1949.

Manning, Brennan. *The Ragamuffin Gospel.* Sisters: Multnomah Books, 1990.

Martin, R. P., and Davids, P. H. *Dictionary of the later New Testament and its Developments.* Downers Grove: InterVarsity Press, 2000.

May, Gerald. *Addictions and Grace.* San Francisco: Harper, 1988.

McDowell, Josh, and Don Stewart. *Handbook of Today's Religions.* San Bernardino: Here's Life Publishers, 1983.

McKnight, Scot. *Community called Atonement.* Nashville: Abingdon Press, 2007.

Meyers, David G. *Psychology 9th Edition.* New York: Worth Publishers, 2010.

Mitchell, Greg W. *"Come Follow Me!" Discovering Whom we are to Follow in Selected Works of Twentieth Century Protestant Theology.* Vancouver: Regent College, 1988.

Niebuhr, H. Richard. *Christ and Culture.* San Francisco: Harper Collins, 1996.

Packer, J. I. *God's Words.* Downers Grove: InterVarsity Press, 1981.

Packer, J. I. *Knowing God.* London: Hodder & Stoughton, 1973.

Reeves, Michael. *Delighting in the Trinity.* Downers Grove: IVP, 2012.

Richard of St. Victor. Translated by Grover A. Zinn, *The Twelve Patriarchs, The Mystical Ark, Book Three of the Trinity.* New York: Paulist Press, 1979.

Rizzuto, Ann-Maria. *The Birth of the Living God.* Chicago: University of Chicago Press, 1979.

Ryrie, Charles C. *What You Should Know About Inerrancy.* Chicago: Moody Press, 1981.

Stewart, Steve. *When Everything Changes.* Abbotsford: Fresh Wind Press, 2012.

Stott, John R. W. *Basic Christianity.* Grand Rapids: Eerdmans, 1988.

Waltke, Bruce K. *An Old Testament Theology.* Grand Rapids: Zondervan, 2007.

Walton, John H. *The Lost World of Genesis One*. Downers Grove: InterVarsity Press, 2009.

Webb, J. *Slaves, Women and Homosexuals*. Downers Grove: InterVarsity Press, 2001.

Wilkerson, Mike. *Redemption*. Wheaton: Crossway, 2011.

Wright, N. T. *Surprised by Hope*, HarperCollins e-books, 2008.

Courses

Barker, Paul. *Life of Faith*, Every Nation Leadership Institute, 2007.

Pratney, Winkey. *The Character of God*. Morning Star School of Campus Ministry, 2003.

Provan, Iain. *Genesis*. Regent College, 2008.

Reagan, David. *Eschatology*. Northwest Graduate School of the Ministry, 1997.

Articles

Beverly, James A., interviewing the high priest of the church of Satan, Peter H. Gilmore. *Faith Today*, May/June 2012.

Cunningham, John D. and John K. Antill. "Cohabitation and Marriage: Retrospective and Predictive Comparisons," Journal of Social and Personal Relationships 11 (1994).

Green, Michael and Gordon Carkner. *10 Myths about Christianity*.

Keller, Timothy. *Hell: Isn't the God of Christianity an Angry Judge?* PreachingToday.com, 2010.

Keller, Timothy. *Preaching the Gospel in a Post-Modern World*, 2002.

Keller, Timothy. *The Gospel Coalition*, May 23, 2007.

Mission Gateway Magazine. Fort Erie: Intercede International, Spring/Summer 2012.

Newsboys. *Lost the Plot* (Album: *Take me to your leader*, 1996).

Olson, Roger. *"Relational Theology"* http://www.patheos.com/blogs/jesuscreed/2013/04/17/

Pinnock, Clark. *The Destruction of the Finally Impenitent*, 1992.

Rising Prevalence of Antidepressants Among US Youths, Journal of the America Academy of Pediatrics, May 2012.

Stephen Mansfield. *Egypt: A Contrarian View*, February 14, 2011.

Waltke, Bruce K. CRUX, Winter 2007/Vol. 43, No. 4. 14. *Ask of me, My Son: Exposition of Psalm 2*.

Walton, John. "Creation in Genesis 1:1-2:3 and the Ancient Near East." (Calvin Theological Journal 43, 2008).

www.canada.com/nationalpost/newsstory.html?id=f97e6516-f8fe48f6-8d81-81a5f607e2de.

www.religioustolerance.org/rel_rate.htm. Nov 06.

Manufactured by Amazon.ca
Bolton, ON

38044106R00107